"In the journal I do not just express myself more openly than I could to any person; I create myself. The journal is a vehicle for my sense of selfhood. It represents me as emotionally and spiritually independent. Therefore (alas) it does not simply record my actual, daily life but rather — in many cases — offers an alternative to it."

— Susan Sontag

How To Use This Journal

Primary Aim Questionnaire

Your **Primary Aim** is one of THE most important things you need to know because it serves as your guide to reaching the best version of yourself. It is essentially your purpose and you must create it intentionally.

In order to discover your Primary Aim, you must decide on what you want your life's reality to be and what you do not want it to be. Then, take a closer look at yourself to see what self-imposing limitations should be eliminated in order to reach those goals.

The questions in this section have been designed to help you clarify exactly what your Primary Aim is. They originate from the book, "The E-Myth" by Michael Gerber. Please answer them carefully, taking time to think deeply about what each one is asking. After completing the questionnaire, you will have a clear understanding of what is important and what is not. Your answers will become the standards you use to measure your life by.

Affirmations

Did you know that an affirmation is really anything you say or think? The word 'affirmation' originates from the Latin word 'affirmare,' which means "to streghthen, to make steady". Therefore, every thought we regularly entertain strengthens certain beliefs.

Research shows, the average person has about 60,000 thoughts a day and of those thoughts, 75% are negative. It's no wonder why we are often surrounded by negative experiences.

In order to change our lives, we have to retrain our thinking and speaking into positive patterns. By repeating positive affirmations throughout your day, you are consciously choosing words that will either help eliminate something from your life or help create something new.

Use the affirmations in this section to start retraining your brain and address personal characteristics you may wish to have or want more of.

Journaling Pages

There are so many benefits to getting your thoughts out of your head and onto paper. Journaling reduces stress, helps clarify thoughts and feelings, increase self-awareness and allows you to solve problems more efficiently. Take 10 minutes in the morning and evening to answer the prompts. With time, your mind and habits will change.

Primary Aim Questionnaire

What do I value most?

What kind of life do I want?

What do I want my life to look and feel like?

Who do I wish to be?

Imagine your family and friends at your funeral. Instead of having a preacher deliver the eulogy, imagine that there will be a tape recording of you telling your life story. How would you want that story to go?

How do I wish my life to be on a day-to-day basis?

What would I like to say I know for sure in my life? about my life?

How would I like to be with other people in my life? (Family, friends, business associates, customers, employees, community)

How would I like people to think about me?

What would I like to be doing 2 years from now? 10 years? 20 years? When my life comes to a close?

What specifically would I like to learn during my life spiritually? physically? financially? technically? intellectually? about relationships?

How much money will I need to do the things I wish to do? By when will I need it?

Affirmations

Use the following affirmations to start retraining your brain and address personal characteristics you may wish to have or want more of. Repeat throughout the day for best results.

Today I am laying the foundation for a wonderful future.
I am the architect of my life. I am the creator of my reality.
I am able to achieve whatever I desire.
This day will bring me nothing but joy, fulfillment and happiness.
I am able to conquer all the challenges I am confronted with.
I am supported and loved by God. My potential to succeed is infinite.
I am the exception to the rule; God's favor always prospers me.
I am creative and bursting with brilliant ideas.
I accept and love myself just the way I am.
New and exciting opportunities manifest in my life all the time.

Increase Health

I am healthy, energetic and optimistic.
Every day I'm getting healthier.
My body is a holy temple. I keep it clean and maintain its functionality.
I enjoy exercising regularly & eating healthy, well-balanced meals.
I have the discipline and self control to achieve and maintain my dream body.

Transcend Feelings of Fear/Anxiety

My body is relaxed. My mind is calm. My soul is at peace.
I am safe and protected by God. Fear is just an emotion. I have nothing to be afraid of.
The challenges I'm confronted with are opportunities for growth.
Every situation serves my highest good.
The future holds all kinds of pleasant surprises.
I let go of worries and replace them with excitement, hope and optimism.
I am not afraid of failure; Failure teaches me how I can become successful in life.
I am courageous and overcome my fears by confronting them.

Increase Self-Worth

I love and accept myself unconditionally.

I forgive myself for all my mistakes, failures and shortcomings.

I am significant, designed with purpose, & contribute to the advancement of humankind.

I am worthy of happiness and love.

I am God's workmanship created to do good works.

Transcend Feelings of Hopelessness/Disgust

Everything happens for a reason. Everything leads to something positive.

I am able to find optimistic ways of dealing with difficulties.

There is good to be found in every situation, even if I may not see it at the moment.

There is always another way. There is always a solution to my problems.

I am at peace with my past and hopeful about my future.

Increase Self Confidence

I radiate confidence, love, happiness, grace and positivity.

I trust in my ability to create a fabulous future and overcome drawbacks.

God placed everything I need to make my dreams a reality inside of me.

I always make sound decisions because God guides me in every situation.

I am bold and courageous in the face of difficulty. Challenges bring out the best in me.

Transcend Feelings of Rejection/Loneliness

I enjoy my own company, it helps me to get in touch with my true self.

I am at peace and happy when I'm alone.

My family and friends support me, even if they don't share my dreams.

I have compassion when others don't understand my viewpoints.

I have all the support and help I need.

Increase Abundance/Prosperity

My life is full of prosperity; I see abundance everywhere.

I attract money effortlessly and easily. God blesses everything I put my hands on.

The more wealth I obtain, the more I bless others.

I continuously discover new avenues of income.

I am a lender and not a borrower; I am the head and not the tail.

Transcend Feelings of Anger

I am patient, long-suffering, and forgiving toward others.

Anger is an emotion that does not solve any problems.

I stay calm in frustrating situations.

I let go of anger because it helps me to make better decisions & see things more clearly.

The compassion & understanding I possess helps me to overcome anger.

Increase Happiness/Gratitude

I am grateful for the wonders in my life.

I am overflowing with happiness, joy and satisfaction.

I am excited to see what the present day holds.

God's grace and love is working through me.

I am able to find positivity and a reason to be thankful in every situation.

Transcend Feelings of Social Awkwardness

I feel relaxed and comfortable around other people.

I enjoy meeting new people. I even seek out others.

I am outgoing. I can enrich other people's lives.

I am easy to talk to & I am confident when I'm around others.

I am a joy to be around and others easily see the value I possess.

Morning

MORNING (DATE:)

TODAY, I AM THANKFUL FOR:
-
-
-
-
-

MY INTENTIONS/GOALS FOR TODAY ARE:
-
-
-

POSSIBLE OBSTACLES:

PREVENTATIVE/CONTINGENCY PLAN:

I WILL EMBODY "LOVE" BY: (SPECIFIC ACTIONS)

I FEEL EXCITED FOR/I FEEL APPREHENSIVE ABOUT:

THOUGHT DOWNLOAD:

Evening

EVENING (DATE:)

THE 1 THING I DID TODAY THAT SCARED ME

TODAY I LEARNED/EXPERIENCED:

I AM PROUD OF MYSELF FOR:

THE THINGS I COULD WORK ON DOING BETTER ARE:

I AM BLESSED BECAUSE:

THOUGHT DOWNLOAD:

Morning

MORNING (DATE:)

MY INTENTIONS/GOALS FOR TODAY ARE:

-
-
-

TODAY, I AM THANKFUL FOR:

-
-
-
-
-

POSSIBLE OBSTACLES:

PREVENTATIVE/CONTINGENCY PLAN:

I WILL EMBODY "LOVE" BY: (SPECIFIC ACTIONS)

I FEEL EXCITED FOR/I FEEL APPREHENSIVE ABOUT:

THOUGHT DOWNLOAD:

Evening

EVENING (DATE:)

THE 1 THING I DID TODAY THAT SCARED ME

TODAY I LEARNED/EXPERIENCED:

I AM PROUD OF MYSELF FOR:

THE THINGS I COULD WORK ON DOING BETTER ARE:

I AM BLESSED BECAUSE:

THOUGHT DOWNLOAD:

Morning

MORNING (DATE:)

MY INTENTIONS/GOALS FOR TODAY ARE:
-
-
-

TODAY, I AM THANKFUL FOR:
-
-
-
-
-

POSSIBLE OBSTACLES:

PREVENTATIVE/CONTINGENCY PLAN:

I WILL EMBODY "LOVE" BY: (SPECIFIC ACTIONS)

I FEEL EXCITED FOR/I FEEL APPREHENSIVE ABOUT:

THOUGHT DOWNLOAD:

Evening

EVENING (DATE:)

THE 1 THING I DID TODAY THAT SCARED ME

TODAY I LEARNED/EXPERIENCED:

I AM PROUD OF MYSELF FOR:

THE THINGS I COULD WORK ON DOING BETTER ARE:

I AM BLESSED BECAUSE:

THOUGHT DOWNLOAD:

Morning

MORNING (DATE:)

TODAY, I AM THANKFUL FOR:
-
-
-
-
-

MY INTENTIONS/GOALS FOR TODAY ARE:
-
-
-

POSSIBLE OBSTACLES:

PREVENTATIVE/CONTINGENCY PLAN:

I WILL EMBODY "LOVE" BY: (SPECIFIC ACTIONS)

I FEEL EXCITED FOR/I FEEL APPREHENSIVE ABOUT:

THOUGHT DOWNLOAD:

Evening

EVENING (DATE:)

THE 1 THING I DID TODAY THAT SCARED ME

TODAY I LEARNED/EXPERIENCED:

I AM PROUD OF MYSELF FOR:

THE THINGS I COULD WORK ON DOING BETTER ARE:

I AM BLESSED BECAUSE:

THOUGHT DOWNLOAD:

Morning

MORNING (DATE:)

MY INTENTIONS/GOALS FOR TODAY ARE:
-
-
-

TODAY, I AM THANKFUL FOR:
-
-
-
-
-

POSSIBLE OBSTACLES:

PREVENTATIVE/CONTINGENCY PLAN:

I WILL EMBODY "LOVE" BY: (SPECIFIC ACTIONS)

I FEEL EXCITED FOR/I FEEL APPREHENSIVE ABOUT:

THOUGHT DOWNLOAD:

Evening

EVENING (DATE:)

THE 1 THING I DID TODAY THAT SCARED ME

TODAY I LEARNED/EXPERIENCED:

I AM PROUD OF MYSELF FOR:

THE THINGS I COULD WORK ON DOING BETTER ARE:

I AM BLESSED BECAUSE:

THOUGHT DOWNLOAD:

Morning

MORNING (DATE:)

MY INTENTIONS/GOALS FOR TODAY ARE:

-
-
-

TODAY, I AM THANKFUL FOR:

-
-
-
-
-

POSSIBLE OBSTACLES:

PREVENTATIVE/CONTINGENCY PLAN:

I WILL EMBODY "LOVE" BY: (SPECIFIC ACTIONS)

I FEEL EXCITED FOR/I FEEL APPREHENSIVE ABOUT:

THOUGHT DOWNLOAD:

Evening

EVENING (DATE:)

THE 1 THING I DID TODAY THAT SCARED ME

TODAY I LEARNED/EXPERIENCED:

I AM PROUD OF MYSELF FOR:

THE THINGS I COULD WORK ON DOING BETTER ARE:

I AM BLESSED BECAUSE:

THOUGHT DOWNLOAD:

Morning

MORNING (DATE:)

MY INTENTIONS/GOALS FOR TODAY ARE:
-
-
-

TODAY, I AM THANKFUL FOR:
-
-
-
-
-

POSSIBLE OBSTACLES:

PREVENTATIVE/CONTINGENCY PLAN:

I WILL EMBODY "LOVE" BY: (SPECIFIC ACTIONS)

I FEEL EXCITED FOR/I FEEL APPREHENSIVE ABOUT:

THOUGHT DOWNLOAD:

Evening

EVENING (DATE:)

THE 1 THING I DID TODAY THAT SCARED ME

TODAY I LEARNED/EXPERIENCED:

I AM PROUD OF MYSELF FOR:

THE THINGS I COULD WORK ON DOING BETTER ARE:

I AM BLESSED BECAUSE:

THOUGHT DOWNLOAD:

Morning

MORNING (DATE:)

MY INTENTIONS/GOALS FOR TODAY ARE:
-
-
-

TODAY, I AM THANKFUL FOR:
-
-
-
-
-

POSSIBLE OBSTACLES:

PREVENTATIVE/CONTINGENCY PLAN:

I WILL EMBODY "LOVE" BY: (SPECIFIC ACTIONS)

I FEEL EXCITED FOR/I FEEL APPREHENSIVE ABOUT:

THOUGHT DOWNLOAD:

Evening

EVENING (DATE:)

THE 1 THING I DID TODAY THAT SCARED ME

TODAY I LEARNED/EXPERIENCED:

I AM PROUD OF MYSELF FOR:

THE THINGS I COULD WORK ON DOING BETTER ARE:

I AM BLESSED BECAUSE:

THOUGHT DOWNLOAD:

Morning

MORNING (DATE:)

MY INTENTIONS/GOALS FOR TODAY ARE:
-
-
-

TODAY, I AM THANKFUL FOR:
-
-
-
-
-

POSSIBLE OBSTACLES:

PREVENTATIVE/CONTINGENCY PLAN:

I WILL EMBODY "LOVE" BY: (SPECIFIC ACTIONS)

I FEEL EXCITED FOR/I FEEL APPREHENSIVE ABOUT:

THOUGHT DOWNLOAD:

Evening

EVENING (DATE:)

THE 1 THING I DID TODAY THAT SCARED ME

TODAY I LEARNED/EXPERIENCED:

I AM PROUD OF MYSELF FOR:

THE THINGS I COULD WORK ON DOING BETTER ARE:

I AM BLESSED BECAUSE:

THOUGHT DOWNLOAD:

Morning

MORNING (DATE:)

MY INTENTIONS/GOALS FOR TODAY ARE:
-
-
-

TODAY, I AM THANKFUL FOR:
-
-
-
-
-

POSSIBLE OBSTACLES:

PREVENTATIVE/CONTINGENCY PLAN:

I WILL EMBODY "LOVE" BY: (SPECIFIC ACTIONS)

I FEEL EXCITED FOR/I FEEL APPREHENSIVE ABOUT:

THOUGHT DOWNLOAD:

Evening

EVENING (DATE:)

THE 1 THING I DID TODAY THAT SCARED ME

TODAY I LEARNED/EXPERIENCED:

I AM PROUD OF MYSELF FOR:

THE THINGS I COULD WORK ON DOING BETTER ARE:

I AM BLESSED BECAUSE:

THOUGHT DOWNLOAD:

Morning

MORNING (DATE:)

MY INTENTIONS/GOALS FOR TODAY ARE:
-
-
-

TODAY, I AM THANKFUL FOR:
-
-
-
-
-

POSSIBLE OBSTACLES:

PREVENTATIVE/CONTINGENCY PLAN:

I WILL EMBODY "LOVE" BY: (SPECIFIC ACTIONS)

I FEEL EXCITED FOR/I FEEL APPREHENSIVE ABOUT:

THOUGHT DOWNLOAD:

Evening

EVENING (DATE:)

THE 1 THING I DID TODAY THAT SCARED ME

TODAY I LEARNED/EXPERIENCED:

I AM PROUD OF MYSELF FOR:

THE THINGS I COULD WORK ON DOING BETTER ARE:

I AM BLESSED BECAUSE:

THOUGHT DOWNLOAD:

Morning

MORNING (DATE:)

MY INTENTIONS/GOALS FOR TODAY ARE:
-
-
-

TODAY, I AM THANKFUL FOR:
-
-
-
-
-

POSSIBLE OBSTACLES:

PREVENTATIVE/CONTINGENCY PLAN:

I WILL EMBODY "LOVE" BY: (SPECIFIC ACTIONS)

I FEEL EXCITED FOR/I FEEL APPREHENSIVE ABOUT:

THOUGHT DOWNLOAD:

Evening

EVENING (DATE:)

THE 1 THING I DID TODAY THAT SCARED ME

TODAY I LEARNED/EXPERIENCED:

I AM PROUD OF MYSELF FOR:

THE THINGS I COULD WORK ON DOING BETTER ARE:

I AM BLESSED BECAUSE:

THOUGHT DOWNLOAD:

Morning

MORNING (DATE:)

MY INTENTIONS/GOALS FOR TODAY ARE:
-
-
-

TODAY, I AM THANKFUL FOR:
-
-
-
-
-

POSSIBLE OBSTACLES:

PREVENTATIVE/CONTINGENCY PLAN:

I WILL EMBODY "LOVE" BY: (SPECIFIC ACTIONS)

I FEEL EXCITED FOR/I FEEL APPREHENSIVE ABOUT:

THOUGHT DOWNLOAD:

Evening

EVENING (DATE:)

THE 1 THING I DID TODAY THAT SCARED ME

TODAY I LEARNED/EXPERIENCED:

I AM PROUD OF MYSELF FOR:

THE THINGS I COULD WORK ON DOING BETTER ARE:

I AM BLESSED BECAUSE:

THOUGHT DOWNLOAD:

Morning

MORNING (DATE:)

MY INTENTIONS/GOALS FOR TODAY ARE:
-
-
-

TODAY, I AM THANKFUL FOR:
-
-
-
-
-

POSSIBLE OBSTACLES:

PREVENTATIVE/CONTINGENCY PLAN:

I WILL EMBODY "LOVE" BY: (SPECIFIC ACTIONS)

I FEEL EXCITED FOR/I FEEL APPREHENSIVE ABOUT:

THOUGHT DOWNLOAD:

Evening

EVENING (DATE:)

THE 1 THING I DID TODAY THAT SCARED ME

TODAY I LEARNED/EXPERIENCED:

I AM PROUD OF MYSELF FOR:

THE THINGS I COULD WORK ON DOING BETTER ARE:

I AM BLESSED BECAUSE:

THOUGHT DOWNLOAD:

Morning

MORNING (DATE:)

MY INTENTIONS/GOALS FOR TODAY ARE:
-
-
-

TODAY, I AM THANKFUL FOR:
-
-
-
-
-

POSSIBLE OBSTACLES:

PREVENTATIVE/CONTINGENCY PLAN:

I WILL EMBODY "LOVE" BY: (SPECIFIC ACTIONS)

I FEEL EXCITED FOR/I FEEL APPREHENSIVE ABOUT:

THOUGHT DOWNLOAD:

Evening

EVENING (DATE:)

THE 1 THING I DID TODAY THAT SCARED ME

TODAY I LEARNED/EXPERIENCED:

I AM PROUD OF MYSELF FOR:

THE THINGS I COULD WORK ON DOING BETTER ARE:

I AM BLESSED BECAUSE:

THOUGHT DOWNLOAD:

Morning

MORNING (DATE:)

MY INTENTIONS/GOALS FOR TODAY ARE:

-
-
-

TODAY, I AM THANKFUL FOR:

-
-
-
-
-

POSSIBLE OBSTACLES:

PREVENTATIVE/CONTINGENCY PLAN:

I WILL EMBODY "LOVE" BY: (SPECIFIC ACTIONS)

I FEEL EXCITED FOR/I FEEL APPREHENSIVE ABOUT:

THOUGHT DOWNLOAD:

Evening

EVENING (DATE:)

THE 1 THING I DID TODAY THAT SCARED ME

TODAY I LEARNED/EXPERIENCED:

I AM PROUD OF MYSELF FOR:

THE THINGS I COULD WORK ON DOING BETTER ARE:

I AM BLESSED BECAUSE:

THOUGHT DOWNLOAD:

Morning

MORNING (DATE:)

MY INTENTIONS/GOALS FOR TODAY ARE:
-
-
-

TODAY, I AM THANKFUL FOR:
-
-
-
-
-

POSSIBLE OBSTACLES:

PREVENTATIVE/CONTINGENCY PLAN:

I WILL EMBODY "LOVE" BY: (SPECIFIC ACTIONS)

I FEEL EXCITED FOR/I FEEL APPREHENSIVE ABOUT:

THOUGHT DOWNLOAD:

Evening

EVENING (DATE:)

THE 1 THING I DID TODAY THAT SCARED ME

TODAY I LEARNED/EXPERIENCED:

I AM PROUD OF MYSELF FOR:

THE THINGS I COULD WORK ON DOING BETTER ARE:

I AM BLESSED BECAUSE:

THOUGHT DOWNLOAD:

Morning

MORNING (DATE:)

MY INTENTIONS/GOALS FOR TODAY ARE:

-
-
-

TODAY, I AM THANKFUL FOR:

-
-
-
-
-

POSSIBLE OBSTACLES:

PREVENTATIVE/CONTINGENCY PLAN:

I WILL EMBODY "LOVE" BY: (SPECIFIC ACTIONS)

I FEEL EXCITED FOR/I FEEL APPREHENSIVE ABOUT:

THOUGHT DOWNLOAD:

Evening

EVENING (DATE:)

THE 1 THING I DID TODAY THAT SCARED ME

TODAY I LEARNED/EXPERIENCED:

I AM PROUD OF MYSELF FOR:

THE THINGS I COULD WORK ON DOING BETTER ARE:

I AM BLESSED BECAUSE:

THOUGHT DOWNLOAD:

Morning

MORNING (DATE:)

TODAY, I AM THANKFUL FOR:
-
-
-
-

MY INTENTIONS/GOALS FOR TODAY ARE:
-
-
-

POSSIBLE OBSTACLES:

PREVENTATIVE/CONTINGENCY PLAN:

I WILL EMBODY "LOVE" BY: (SPECIFIC ACTIONS)

I FEEL EXCITED FOR/I FEEL APPREHENSIVE ABOUT:

THOUGHT DOWNLOAD:

Evening

EVENING (DATE:)

THE 1 THING I DID TODAY THAT SCARED ME

TODAY I LEARNED/EXPERIENCED:

I AM PROUD OF MYSELF FOR:

THE THINGS I COULD WORK ON DOING BETTER ARE:

I AM BLESSED BECAUSE:

THOUGHT DOWNLOAD:

Morning

MORNING (DATE:)

MY INTENTIONS/GOALS FOR TODAY ARE:
-
-
-

TODAY, I AM THANKFUL FOR:
-
-
-
-
-

POSSIBLE OBSTACLES:

PREVENTATIVE/CONTINGENCY PLAN:

I WILL EMBODY "LOVE" BY: (SPECIFIC ACTIONS)

I FEEL EXCITED FOR/I FEEL APPREHENSIVE ABOUT:

THOUGHT DOWNLOAD:

Evening

EVENING (DATE:)

THE 1 THING I DID TODAY THAT SCARED ME

TODAY I LEARNED/EXPERIENCED:

I AM PROUD OF MYSELF FOR:

THE THINGS I COULD WORK ON DOING BETTER ARE:

I AM BLESSED BECAUSE:

THOUGHT DOWNLOAD:

Morning

MORNING (DATE:)

MY INTENTIONS/GOALS FOR TODAY ARE:
-
-
-

TODAY, I AM THANKFUL FOR:
-
-
-
-
-

POSSIBLE OBSTACLES:

PREVENTATIVE/CONTINGENCY PLAN:

I WILL EMBODY "LOVE" BY: (SPECIFIC ACTIONS)

I FEEL EXCITED FOR/I FEEL APPREHENSIVE ABOUT:

THOUGHT DOWNLOAD:

Evening

EVENING (DATE:)

THE 1 THING I DID TODAY THAT SCARED ME

TODAY I LEARNED/EXPERIENCED:

I AM PROUD OF MYSELF FOR:

THE THINGS I COULD WORK ON DOING BETTER ARE:

I AM BLESSED BECAUSE:

THOUGHT DOWNLOAD:

Morning

MORNING (DATE:)

TODAY, I AM THANKFUL FOR:
-
-
-
-
-

MY INTENTIONS/GOALS FOR TODAY ARE:
-
-
-

POSSIBLE OBSTACLES:

PREVENTATIVE/CONTINGENCY PLAN:

I WILL EMBODY "LOVE" BY: (SPECIFIC ACTIONS)

I FEEL EXCITED FOR/I FEEL APPREHENSIVE ABOUT:

THOUGHT DOWNLOAD:

Evening

EVENING (DATE:)

THE 1 THING I DID TODAY THAT SCARED ME

TODAY I LEARNED/EXPERIENCED:

I AM PROUD OF MYSELF FOR:

THE THINGS I COULD WORK ON DOING BETTER ARE:

I AM BLESSED BECAUSE:

THOUGHT DOWNLOAD:

Morning

MORNING (DATE:)

TODAY, I AM THANKFUL FOR:
-
-
-
-

MY INTENTIONS/GOALS FOR TODAY ARE:
-
-
-

POSSIBLE OBSTACLES:

PREVENTATIVE/CONTINGENCY PLAN:

I WILL EMBODY "LOVE" BY: (SPECIFIC ACTIONS)

I FEEL EXCITED FOR/I FEEL APPREHENSIVE ABOUT:

THOUGHT DOWNLOAD:

Evening

EVENING (DATE:)

THE 1 THING I DID TODAY THAT SCARED ME

TODAY I LEARNED/EXPERIENCED:

I AM PROUD OF MYSELF FOR:

THE THINGS I COULD WORK ON DOING BETTER ARE:

I AM BLESSED BECAUSE:

THOUGHT DOWNLOAD:

Morning

MORNING (DATE:)

MY INTENTIONS/GOALS FOR TODAY ARE:
-
-
-

TODAY, I AM THANKFUL FOR:
-
-
-
-
-

POSSIBLE OBSTACLES:

PREVENTATIVE/CONTINGENCY PLAN:

I WILL EMBODY "LOVE" BY: (SPECIFIC ACTIONS)

I FEEL EXCITED FOR/I FEEL APPREHENSIVE ABOUT:

THOUGHT DOWNLOAD:

Evening

EVENING (DATE:)

THE 1 THING I DID TODAY THAT SCARED ME

TODAY I LEARNED/EXPERIENCED:

I AM PROUD OF MYSELF FOR:

THE THINGS I COULD WORK ON DOING BETTER ARE:

I AM BLESSED BECAUSE:

THOUGHT DOWNLOAD:

Morning

MORNING (DATE:)

MY INTENTIONS/GOALS FOR TODAY ARE:
-
-
-

TODAY, I AM THANKFUL FOR:
-
-
-
-
-

POSSIBLE OBSTACLES:

PREVENTATIVE/CONTINGENCY PLAN:

I WILL EMBODY "LOVE" BY: (SPECIFIC ACTIONS)

I FEEL EXCITED FOR/I FEEL APPREHENSIVE ABOUT:

THOUGHT DOWNLOAD:

Evening

EVENING (DATE:)

THE 1 THING I DID TODAY THAT SCARED ME

TODAY I LEARNED/EXPERIENCED:

I AM PROUD OF MYSELF FOR:

THE THINGS I COULD WORK ON DOING BETTER ARE:

I AM BLESSED BECAUSE:

THOUGHT DOWNLOAD:

Morning

MORNING (DATE:)

MY INTENTIONS/GOALS FOR TODAY ARE:
-
-
-

TODAY, I AM THANKFUL FOR:
-
-
-
-
-

POSSIBLE OBSTACLES:

PREVENTATIVE/CONTINGENCY PLAN:

I WILL EMBODY "LOVE" BY: (SPECIFIC ACTIONS)

I FEEL EXCITED FOR/I FEEL APPREHENSIVE ABOUT:

THOUGHT DOWNLOAD:

Evening

EVENING (DATE:)

THE 1 THING I DID TODAY THAT SCARED ME

TODAY I LEARNED/EXPERIENCED:

I AM PROUD OF MYSELF FOR:

THE THINGS I COULD WORK ON DOING BETTER ARE:

I AM BLESSED BECAUSE:

THOUGHT DOWNLOAD:

Morning

MORNING (DATE:)

TODAY, I AM THANKFUL FOR:
-
-
-
-
-

MY INTENTIONS/GOALS FOR TODAY ARE:
-
-
-

POSSIBLE OBSTACLES:

PREVENTATIVE/CONTINGENCY PLAN:

I WILL EMBODY "LOVE" BY: (SPECIFIC ACTIONS)

I FEEL EXCITED FOR/I FEEL APPREHENSIVE ABOUT:

THOUGHT DOWNLOAD:

Evening

EVENING (DATE:)

THE 1 THING I DID TODAY THAT SCARED ME

TODAY I LEARNED/EXPERIENCED:

I AM PROUD OF MYSELF FOR:

THE THINGS I COULD WORK ON DOING BETTER ARE:

I AM BLESSED BECAUSE:

THOUGHT DOWNLOAD:

Morning

MORNING (DATE:)

MY INTENTIONS/GOALS FOR TODAY ARE:
-
-
-

TODAY, I AM THANKFUL FOR:
-
-
-
-
-

POSSIBLE OBSTACLES:

PREVENTATIVE/CONTINGENCY PLAN:

I WILL EMBODY "LOVE" BY: (SPECIFIC ACTIONS)

I FEEL EXCITED FOR/I FEEL APPREHENSIVE ABOUT:

THOUGHT DOWNLOAD:

Evening

EVENING (DATE:)

THE 1 THING I DID TODAY THAT SCARED ME

TODAY I LEARNED/EXPERIENCED:

I AM PROUD OF MYSELF FOR:

THE THINGS I COULD WORK ON DOING BETTER ARE:

I AM BLESSED BECAUSE:

THOUGHT DOWNLOAD:

Morning

MORNING (DATE:)

TODAY, I AM THANKFUL FOR:
-
-
-
-

MY INTENTIONS/GOALS FOR TODAY ARE:
-
-
-

POSSIBLE OBSTACLES:

PREVENTATIVE/CONTINGENCY PLAN:

I WILL EMBODY "LOVE" BY: (SPECIFIC ACTIONS)

I FEEL EXCITED FOR/I FEEL APPREHENSIVE ABOUT:

THOUGHT DOWNLOAD:

Evening

EVENING (DATE:)

THE 1 THING I DID TODAY THAT SCARED ME

TODAY I LEARNED/EXPERIENCED:

I AM PROUD OF MYSELF FOR:

THE THINGS I COULD WORK ON DOING BETTER ARE:

I AM BLESSED BECAUSE:

THOUGHT DOWNLOAD:

Morning

MORNING (DATE:)

TODAY, I AM THANKFUL FOR:
-
-
-
-
-

MY INTENTIONS/GOALS FOR TODAY ARE:
-
-
-

POSSIBLE OBSTACLES:

PREVENTATIVE/CONTINGENCY PLAN:

I WILL EMBODY "LOVE" BY: (SPECIFIC ACTIONS)

I FEEL EXCITED FOR/I FEEL APPREHENSIVE ABOUT:

THOUGHT DOWNLOAD:

Evening

EVENING (DATE:)

THE 1 THING I DID TODAY THAT SCARED ME

TODAY I LEARNED/EXPERIENCED:

I AM PROUD OF MYSELF FOR:

THE THINGS I COULD WORK ON DOING BETTER ARE:

I AM BLESSED BECAUSE:

THOUGHT DOWNLOAD:

Morning

MORNING (DATE:)

MY INTENTIONS/GOALS FOR TODAY ARE:
-
-
-

TODAY, I AM THANKFUL FOR:
-
-
-
-

POSSIBLE OBSTACLES:

PREVENTATIVE/CONTINGENCY PLAN:

I WILL EMBODY "LOVE" BY: (SPECIFIC ACTIONS)

I FEEL EXCITED FOR/I FEEL APPREHENSIVE ABOUT:

THOUGHT DOWNLOAD:

Evening

EVENING (DATE:)

THE 1 THING I DID TODAY THAT SCARED ME

TODAY I LEARNED/EXPERIENCED:

I AM PROUD OF MYSELF FOR:

THE THINGS I COULD WORK ON DOING BETTER ARE:

I AM BLESSED BECAUSE:

THOUGHT DOWNLOAD:

Morning

MORNING (DATE:)

MY INTENTIONS/GOALS FOR TODAY ARE:
-
-
-

TODAY, I AM THANKFUL FOR:
-
-
-
-
-

POSSIBLE OBSTACLES:

PREVENTATIVE/CONTINGENCY PLAN:

I WILL EMBODY "LOVE" BY: (SPECIFIC ACTIONS)

I FEEL EXCITED FOR/I FEEL APPREHENSIVE ABOUT:

THOUGHT DOWNLOAD:

Evening

EVENING (DATE:)

THE 1 THING I DID TODAY THAT SCARED ME

TODAY I LEARNED/EXPERIENCED:

I AM PROUD OF MYSELF FOR:

THE THINGS I COULD WORK ON DOING BETTER ARE:

I AM BLESSED BECAUSE:

THOUGHT DOWNLOAD:

Morning

MORNING (DATE:)

TODAY, I AM THANKFUL FOR:
-
-
-
-
-

MY INTENTIONS/GOALS FOR TODAY ARE:
-
-
-

POSSIBLE OBSTACLES:

PREVENTATIVE/CONTINGENCY PLAN:

I WILL EMBODY "LOVE" BY: (SPECIFIC ACTIONS)

I FEEL EXCITED FOR/I FEEL APPREHENSIVE ABOUT:

THOUGHT DOWNLOAD:

Evening

EVENING (DATE:)

THE 1 THING I DID TODAY THAT SCARED ME

TODAY I LEARNED/EXPERIENCED:

I AM PROUD OF MYSELF FOR:

THE THINGS I COULD WORK ON DOING BETTER ARE:

I AM BLESSED BECAUSE:

THOUGHT DOWNLOAD:

Morning

MORNING (DATE:)

MY INTENTIONS/GOALS FOR TODAY ARE:
-
-
-

TODAY, I AM THANKFUL FOR:
-
-
-
-
-

POSSIBLE OBSTACLES:

PREVENTATIVE/CONTINGENCY PLAN:

I WILL EMBODY "LOVE" BY: (SPECIFIC ACTIONS)

I FEEL EXCITED FOR/I FEEL APPREHENSIVE ABOUT:

THOUGHT DOWNLOAD:

Evening

EVENING (DATE:)

THE 1 THING I DID TODAY THAT SCARED ME

TODAY I LEARNED/EXPERIENCED:

I AM PROUD OF MYSELF FOR:

THE THINGS I COULD WORK ON DOING BETTER ARE:

I AM BLESSED BECAUSE:

THOUGHT DOWNLOAD:

Morning

MORNING (DATE:)

MY INTENTIONS/GOALS FOR TODAY ARE:
-
-
-

TODAY, I AM THANKFUL FOR:
-
-
-
-

POSSIBLE OBSTACLES:

PREVENTATIVE/CONTINGENCY PLAN:

I WILL EMBODY "LOVE" BY: (SPECIFIC ACTIONS)

I FEEL EXCITED FOR/I FEEL APPREHENSIVE ABOUT:

THOUGHT DOWNLOAD:

Evening

EVENING (DATE:)

THE 1 THING I DID TODAY THAT SCARED ME

TODAY I LEARNED/EXPERIENCED:

I AM PROUD OF MYSELF FOR:

THE THINGS I COULD WORK ON DOING BETTER ARE:

I AM BLESSED BECAUSE:

THOUGHT DOWNLOAD:

Morning

MORNING (DATE:)

MY INTENTIONS/GOALS FOR TODAY ARE:
-
-
-

TODAY, I AM THANKFUL FOR:
-
-
-
-
-

POSSIBLE OBSTACLES:

PREVENTATIVE/CONTINGENCY PLAN:

I WILL EMBODY "LOVE" BY: (SPECIFIC ACTIONS)

I FEEL EXCITED FOR/I FEEL APPREHENSIVE ABOUT:

THOUGHT DOWNLOAD:

Evening

EVENING (DATE:)

THE 1 THING I DID TODAY THAT SCARED ME

TODAY I LEARNED/EXPERIENCED:

I AM PROUD OF MYSELF FOR:

THE THINGS I COULD WORK ON DOING BETTER ARE:

I AM BLESSED BECAUSE:

THOUGHT DOWNLOAD:

Morning

MORNING (DATE:)

TODAY, I AM THANKFUL FOR:
-
-
-
-
-

MY INTENTIONS/GOALS FOR TODAY ARE:
-
-
-

POSSIBLE OBSTACLES:

PREVENTATIVE/CONTINGENCY PLAN:

I WILL EMBODY "LOVE" BY: (SPECIFIC ACTIONS)

I FEEL EXCITED FOR/I FEEL APPREHENSIVE ABOUT:

THOUGHT DOWNLOAD:

Evening

EVENING (DATE:)

THE 1 THING I DID TODAY THAT SCARED ME

TODAY I LEARNED/EXPERIENCED:

I AM PROUD OF MYSELF FOR:

THE THINGS I COULD WORK ON DOING BETTER ARE:

I AM BLESSED BECAUSE:

THOUGHT DOWNLOAD:

Morning

MORNING (DATE:)

MY INTENTIONS/GOALS FOR TODAY ARE:
-
-
-

TODAY, I AM THANKFUL FOR:
-
-
-
-
-

POSSIBLE OBSTACLES:

PREVENTATIVE/CONTINGENCY PLAN:

I WILL EMBODY "LOVE" BY: (SPECIFIC ACTIONS)

I FEEL EXCITED FOR/I FEEL APPREHENSIVE ABOUT:

THOUGHT DOWNLOAD:

Evening

EVENING (DATE:)

THE 1 THING I DID TODAY THAT SCARED ME

TODAY I LEARNED/EXPERIENCED:

I AM PROUD OF MYSELF FOR:

THE THINGS I COULD WORK ON DOING BETTER ARE:

I AM BLESSED BECAUSE:

THOUGHT DOWNLOAD:

Morning

MORNING (DATE:)

MY INTENTIONS/GOALS FOR TODAY ARE:
-
-
-

TODAY, I AM THANKFUL FOR:
-
-
-
-
-

POSSIBLE OBSTACLES:

PREVENTATIVE/CONTINGENCY PLAN:

I WILL EMBODY "LOVE" BY: (SPECIFIC ACTIONS)

I FEEL EXCITED FOR/I FEEL APPREHENSIVE ABOUT:

THOUGHT DOWNLOAD:

Evening

EVENING (DATE:)

THE 1 THING I DID TODAY THAT SCARED ME

TODAY I LEARNED/EXPERIENCED:

I AM PROUD OF MYSELF FOR:

THE THINGS I COULD WORK ON DOING BETTER ARE:

I AM BLESSED BECAUSE:

THOUGHT DOWNLOAD:

Morning

MORNING (DATE:)

MY INTENTIONS/GOALS FOR TODAY ARE:
-
-
-

TODAY, I AM THANKFUL FOR:
-
-
-
-
-

POSSIBLE OBSTACLES:

PREVENTATIVE/CONTINGENCY PLAN:

I WILL EMBODY "LOVE" BY: (SPECIFIC ACTIONS)

I FEEL EXCITED FOR/I FEEL APPREHENSIVE ABOUT:

THOUGHT DOWNLOAD:

Evening

EVENING (DATE:)

THE 1 THING I DID TODAY THAT SCARED ME

TODAY I LEARNED/EXPERIENCED:

I AM PROUD OF MYSELF FOR:

THE THINGS I COULD WORK ON DOING BETTER ARE:

I AM BLESSED BECAUSE:

THOUGHT DOWNLOAD:

Morning

MORNING (DATE:)

TODAY, I AM THANKFUL FOR:
-
-
-
-
-

MY INTENTIONS/GOALS FOR TODAY ARE:
-
-
-

POSSIBLE OBSTACLES:

PREVENTATIVE/CONTINGENCY PLAN:

I WILL EMBODY "LOVE" BY: (SPECIFIC ACTIONS)

I FEEL EXCITED FOR/I FEEL APPREHENSIVE ABOUT:

THOUGHT DOWNLOAD:

Evening

EVENING (DATE:)

THE 1 THING I DID TODAY THAT SCARED ME

TODAY I LEARNED/EXPERIENCED:

I AM PROUD OF MYSELF FOR:

THE THINGS I COULD WORK ON DOING BETTER ARE:

I AM BLESSED BECAUSE:

THOUGHT DOWNLOAD:

Morning

MORNING (DATE:)

MY INTENTIONS/GOALS FOR TODAY ARE:
-
-
-

TODAY, I AM THANKFUL FOR:
-
-
-
-
-

POSSIBLE OBSTACLES:

PREVENTATIVE/CONTINGENCY PLAN:

I WILL EMBODY "LOVE" BY: (SPECIFIC ACTIONS)

I FEEL EXCITED FOR/I FEEL APPREHENSIVE ABOUT:

THOUGHT DOWNLOAD:

Evening

EVENING (DATE:)

THE 1 THING I DID TODAY THAT SCARED ME

TODAY I LEARNED/EXPERIENCED:

I AM PROUD OF MYSELF FOR:

THE THINGS I COULD WORK ON DOING BETTER ARE:

I AM BLESSED BECAUSE:

THOUGHT DOWNLOAD:

Morning

MORNING (DATE:)

MY INTENTIONS/GOALS FOR TODAY ARE:
-
-
-

TODAY, I AM THANKFUL FOR:
-
-
-
-
-

POSSIBLE OBSTACLES:

PREVENTATIVE/CONTINGENCY PLAN:

I WILL EMBODY "LOVE" BY: (SPECIFIC ACTIONS)

I FEEL EXCITED FOR/I FEEL APPREHENSIVE ABOUT:

THOUGHT DOWNLOAD:

Evening

EVENING (DATE:)

THE 1 THING I DID TODAY THAT SCARED ME

TODAY I LEARNED/EXPERIENCED:

I AM PROUD OF MYSELF FOR:

THE THINGS I COULD WORK ON DOING BETTER ARE:

I AM BLESSED BECAUSE:

THOUGHT DOWNLOAD:

Morning

MORNING (DATE:)

MY INTENTIONS/GOALS FOR TODAY ARE:

-
-
-

TODAY, I AM THANKFUL FOR:

-
-
-
-
-

POSSIBLE OBSTACLES:

PREVENTATIVE/CONTINGENCY PLAN:

I WILL EMBODY "LOVE" BY: (SPECIFIC ACTIONS)

I FEEL EXCITED FOR/I FEEL APPREHENSIVE ABOUT:

THOUGHT DOWNLOAD:

Evening

EVENING (DATE:)

THE 1 THING I DID TODAY THAT SCARED ME

TODAY I LEARNED/EXPERIENCED:

I AM PROUD OF MYSELF FOR:

THE THINGS I COULD WORK ON DOING BETTER ARE:

I AM BLESSED BECAUSE:

THOUGHT DOWNLOAD:

Morning

MORNING (DATE:)

TODAY, I AM THANKFUL FOR:
-
-
-
-
-

MY INTENTIONS/GOALS FOR TODAY ARE:
-
-
-

POSSIBLE OBSTACLES:

PREVENTATIVE/CONTINGENCY PLAN:

I WILL EMBODY "LOVE" BY: (SPECIFIC ACTIONS)

I FEEL EXCITED FOR/I FEEL APPREHENSIVE ABOUT:

THOUGHT DOWNLOAD:

Evening

EVENING (DATE:)

THE 1 THING I DID TODAY THAT SCARED ME

TODAY I LEARNED/EXPERIENCED:

I AM PROUD OF MYSELF FOR:

THE THINGS I COULD WORK ON DOING BETTER ARE:

I AM BLESSED BECAUSE:

THOUGHT DOWNLOAD:

Morning

MORNING (DATE:)

MY INTENTIONS/GOALS FOR TODAY ARE:
-
-
-

TODAY, I AM THANKFUL FOR:
-
-
-
-
-

POSSIBLE OBSTACLES:

PREVENTATIVE/CONTINGENCY PLAN:

I WILL EMBODY "LOVE" BY: (SPECIFIC ACTIONS)

I FEEL EXCITED FOR/I FEEL APPREHENSIVE ABOUT:

THOUGHT DOWNLOAD:

Evening

EVENING (DATE:)

THE 1 THING I DID TODAY THAT SCARED ME

TODAY I LEARNED/EXPERIENCED:

I AM PROUD OF MYSELF FOR:

THE THINGS I COULD WORK ON DOING BETTER ARE:

I AM BLESSED BECAUSE:

THOUGHT DOWNLOAD:

Morning

MORNING (DATE:)

MY INTENTIONS/GOALS FOR TODAY ARE:
-
-
-

TODAY, I AM THANKFUL FOR:
-
-
-
-
-

POSSIBLE OBSTACLES:

PREVENTATIVE/CONTINGENCY PLAN:

I WILL EMBODY "LOVE" BY: (SPECIFIC ACTIONS)

I FEEL EXCITED FOR/I FEEL APPREHENSIVE ABOUT:

THOUGHT DOWNLOAD:

Evening

EVENING (DATE:)

THE 1 THING I DID TODAY THAT SCARED ME

TODAY I LEARNED/EXPERIENCED:

I AM PROUD OF MYSELF FOR:

THE THINGS I COULD WORK ON DOING BETTER ARE:

I AM BLESSED BECAUSE:

THOUGHT DOWNLOAD:

Morning

MORNING (DATE:)

MY INTENTIONS/GOALS FOR TODAY ARE:
-
-
-

TODAY, I AM THANKFUL FOR:
-
-
-
-
-

POSSIBLE OBSTACLES:

PREVENTATIVE/CONTINGENCY PLAN:

I WILL EMBODY "LOVE" BY: (SPECIFIC ACTIONS)

I FEEL EXCITED FOR/I FEEL APPREHENSIVE ABOUT:

THOUGHT DOWNLOAD:

Evening

EVENING (DATE:)

THE 1 THING I DID TODAY THAT SCARED ME

TODAY I LEARNED/EXPERIENCED:

I AM PROUD OF MYSELF FOR:

THE THINGS I COULD WORK ON DOING BETTER ARE:

I AM BLESSED BECAUSE:

THOUGHT DOWNLOAD:

Morning

MORNING (DATE:)

TODAY, I AM THANKFUL FOR:
-
-
-
-
-

MY INTENTIONS/GOALS FOR TODAY ARE:
-
-
-

POSSIBLE OBSTACLES:

PREVENTATIVE/CONTINGENCY PLAN:

I WILL EMBODY "LOVE" BY: (SPECIFIC ACTIONS)

I FEEL EXCITED FOR/I FEEL APPREHENSIVE ABOUT:

THOUGHT DOWNLOAD:

Evening

EVENING (DATE:)

THE 1 THING I DID TODAY THAT SCARED ME

TODAY I LEARNED/EXPERIENCED:

I AM PROUD OF MYSELF FOR:

THE THINGS I COULD WORK ON DOING BETTER ARE:

I AM BLESSED BECAUSE:

THOUGHT DOWNLOAD:

Morning

MORNING (DATE:)

MY INTENTIONS/GOALS FOR TODAY ARE:
-
-
-

TODAY, I AM THANKFUL FOR:
-
-
-
-
-

POSSIBLE OBSTACLES:

PREVENTATIVE/CONTINGENCY PLAN:

I WILL EMBODY "LOVE" BY: (SPECIFIC ACTIONS)

I FEEL EXCITED FOR/I FEEL APPREHENSIVE ABOUT:

THOUGHT DOWNLOAD:

Evening

EVENING (DATE:)

THE 1 THING I DID TODAY THAT SCARED ME

TODAY I LEARNED/EXPERIENCED:

I AM PROUD OF MYSELF FOR:

THE THINGS I COULD WORK ON DOING BETTER ARE:

I AM BLESSED BECAUSE:

THOUGHT DOWNLOAD:

Morning

MORNING (DATE:)

MY INTENTIONS/GOALS FOR TODAY ARE:
-
-
-

TODAY, I AM THANKFUL FOR:
-
-
-
-
-

POSSIBLE OBSTACLES:

PREVENTATIVE/CONTINGENCY PLAN:

I WILL EMBODY "LOVE" BY: (SPECIFIC ACTIONS)

I FEEL EXCITED FOR/I FEEL APPREHENSIVE ABOUT:

THOUGHT DOWNLOAD:

Evening

EVENING (DATE:)

THE 1 THING I DID TODAY THAT SCARED ME

TODAY I LEARNED/EXPERIENCED:

I AM PROUD OF MYSELF FOR:

THE THINGS I COULD WORK ON DOING BETTER ARE:

I AM BLESSED BECAUSE:

THOUGHT DOWNLOAD:

Morning

MORNING (DATE:)

MY INTENTIONS/GOALS FOR TODAY ARE:

-
-
-

TODAY, I AM THANKFUL FOR:

-
-
-
-
-

POSSIBLE OBSTACLES:

PREVENTATIVE/CONTINGENCY PLAN:

I WILL EMBODY "LOVE" BY: (SPECIFIC ACTIONS)

I FEEL EXCITED FOR/I FEEL APPREHENSIVE ABOUT:

THOUGHT DOWNLOAD:

Evening

EVENING (DATE:)

THE 1 THING I DID TODAY THAT SCARED ME

TODAY I LEARNED/EXPERIENCED:

I AM PROUD OF MYSELF FOR:

THE THINGS I COULD WORK ON DOING BETTER ARE:

I AM BLESSED BECAUSE:

THOUGHT DOWNLOAD:

Morning

MORNING (DATE:)

MY INTENTIONS/GOALS FOR TODAY ARE:
-
-
-

TODAY, I AM THANKFUL FOR:
-
-
-
-
-

POSSIBLE OBSTACLES:

PREVENTATIVE/CONTINGENCY PLAN:

I WILL EMBODY "LOVE" BY: (SPECIFIC ACTIONS)

I FEEL EXCITED FOR/I FEEL APPREHENSIVE ABOUT:

THOUGHT DOWNLOAD:

Evening

EVENING (DATE:)

THE 1 THING I DID TODAY THAT SCARED ME

TODAY I LEARNED/EXPERIENCED:

I AM PROUD OF MYSELF FOR:

THE THINGS I COULD WORK ON DOING BETTER ARE:

I AM BLESSED BECAUSE:

THOUGHT DOWNLOAD:

Morning

MORNING (DATE:)

TODAY, I AM THANKFUL FOR:
-
-
-
-

MY INTENTIONS/GOALS FOR TODAY ARE:
-
-
-

POSSIBLE OBSTACLES:

PREVENTATIVE/CONTINGENCY PLAN:

I WILL EMBODY "LOVE" BY: (SPECIFIC ACTIONS)

I FEEL EXCITED FOR/I FEEL APPREHENSIVE ABOUT:

THOUGHT DOWNLOAD:

Evening

EVENING (DATE:)

THE 1 THING I DID TODAY THAT SCARED ME

TODAY I LEARNED/EXPERIENCED:

I AM PROUD OF MYSELF FOR:

THE THINGS I COULD WORK ON DOING BETTER ARE:

I AM BLESSED BECAUSE:

THOUGHT DOWNLOAD:

Morning

MORNING (DATE:)

MY INTENTIONS/GOALS FOR TODAY ARE:
-
-
-

TODAY, I AM THANKFUL FOR:
-
-
-
-
-

POSSIBLE OBSTACLES:

PREVENTATIVE/CONTINGENCY PLAN:

I WILL EMBODY "LOVE" BY: (SPECIFIC ACTIONS)

I FEEL EXCITED FOR/I FEEL APPREHENSIVE ABOUT:

THOUGHT DOWNLOAD:

Evening

EVENING (DATE:)

THE 1 THING I DID TODAY THAT SCARED ME

TODAY I LEARNED/EXPERIENCED:

I AM PROUD OF MYSELF FOR:

THE THINGS I COULD WORK ON DOING BETTER ARE:

I AM BLESSED BECAUSE:

THOUGHT DOWNLOAD:

Morning

MORNING (DATE:)

MY INTENTIONS/GOALS FOR TODAY ARE:

-
-
-

TODAY, I AM THANKFUL FOR:

-
-
-
-
-

POSSIBLE OBSTACLES:

PREVENTATIVE/CONTINGENCY PLAN:

I WILL EMBODY "LOVE" BY: (SPECIFIC ACTIONS)

I FEEL EXCITED FOR/I FEEL APPREHENSIVE ABOUT:

THOUGHT DOWNLOAD:

Evening

EVENING (DATE:)

THE 1 THING I DID TODAY THAT SCARED ME

TODAY I LEARNED/EXPERIENCED:

I AM PROUD OF MYSELF FOR:

THE THINGS I COULD WORK ON DOING BETTER ARE:

I AM BLESSED BECAUSE:

THOUGHT DOWNLOAD:

Morning

MORNING (DATE:)

MY INTENTIONS/GOALS FOR TODAY ARE:

-
-
-

TODAY, I AM THANKFUL FOR:

-
-
-
-
-

POSSIBLE OBSTACLES:

PREVENTATIVE/CONTINGENCY PLAN:

I WILL EMBODY "LOVE" BY: (SPECIFIC ACTIONS)

I FEEL EXCITED FOR/I FEEL APPREHENSIVE ABOUT:

THOUGHT DOWNLOAD:

Evening

EVENING (DATE:)

THE 1 THING I DID TODAY THAT SCARED ME

TODAY I LEARNED/EXPERIENCED:

I AM PROUD OF MYSELF FOR:

THE THINGS I COULD WORK ON DOING BETTER ARE:

I AM BLESSED BECAUSE:

THOUGHT DOWNLOAD:

Morning

MORNING (DATE:)

MY INTENTIONS/GOALS FOR TODAY ARE:
-
-
-

TODAY, I AM THANKFUL FOR:
-
-
-
-
-

POSSIBLE OBSTACLES:

PREVENTATIVE/CONTINGENCY PLAN:

I WILL EMBODY "LOVE" BY: (SPECIFIC ACTIONS)

I FEEL EXCITED FOR/I FEEL APPREHENSIVE ABOUT:

THOUGHT DOWNLOAD:

Evening

EVENING (DATE:)

THE 1 THING I DID TODAY THAT SCARED ME

TODAY I LEARNED/EXPERIENCED:

I AM PROUD OF MYSELF FOR:

THE THINGS I COULD WORK ON DOING BETTER ARE:

I AM BLESSED BECAUSE:

THOUGHT DOWNLOAD:

Morning

MORNING (DATE:)

MY INTENTIONS/GOALS FOR TODAY ARE:
-
-
-

TODAY, I AM THANKFUL FOR:
-
-
-
-
-

POSSIBLE OBSTACLES:

PREVENTATIVE/CONTINGENCY PLAN:

I WILL EMBODY "LOVE" BY: (SPECIFIC ACTIONS)

I FEEL EXCITED FOR/I FEEL APPREHENSIVE ABOUT:

THOUGHT DOWNLOAD:

Evening

EVENING (DATE:)

THE 1 THING I DID TODAY THAT SCARED ME

TODAY I LEARNED/EXPERIENCED:

I AM PROUD OF MYSELF FOR:

THE THINGS I COULD WORK ON DOING BETTER ARE:

I AM BLESSED BECAUSE:

THOUGHT DOWNLOAD:

Morning

MORNING (DATE:)

MY INTENTIONS/GOALS FOR TODAY ARE:

-
-
-

TODAY, I AM THANKFUL FOR:

-
-
-
-
-

POSSIBLE OBSTACLES:

PREVENTATIVE/CONTINGENCY PLAN:

I WILL EMBODY "LOVE" BY: (SPECIFIC ACTIONS)

I FEEL EXCITED FOR/I FEEL APPREHENSIVE ABOUT:

THOUGHT DOWNLOAD:

Evening

EVENING (DATE:)

THE 1 THING I DID TODAY THAT SCARED ME

TODAY I LEARNED/EXPERIENCED:

I AM PROUD OF MYSELF FOR:

THE THINGS I COULD WORK ON DOING BETTER ARE:

I AM BLESSED BECAUSE:

THOUGHT DOWNLOAD:

Morning

MORNING (DATE:)

MY INTENTIONS/GOALS FOR TODAY ARE:
-
-
-

TODAY, I AM THANKFUL FOR:
-
-
-
-
-

POSSIBLE OBSTACLES:

PREVENTATIVE/CONTINGENCY PLAN:

I WILL EMBODY "LOVE" BY: (SPECIFIC ACTIONS)

I FEEL EXCITED FOR/I FEEL APPREHENSIVE ABOUT:

THOUGHT DOWNLOAD:

Evening

EVENING (DATE:)

THE 1 THING I DID TODAY THAT SCARED ME

TODAY I LEARNED/EXPERIENCED:

I AM PROUD OF MYSELF FOR:

THE THINGS I COULD WORK ON DOING BETTER ARE:

I AM BLESSED BECAUSE:

THOUGHT DOWNLOAD:

Morning

MORNING (DATE:)

TODAY, I AM THANKFUL FOR:
-
-
-
-

MY INTENTIONS/GOALS FOR TODAY ARE:
-
-
-

POSSIBLE OBSTACLES:

PREVENTATIVE/CONTINGENCY PLAN:

I WILL EMBODY "LOVE" BY: (SPECIFIC ACTIONS)

I FEEL EXCITED FOR/I FEEL APPREHENSIVE ABOUT:

THOUGHT DOWNLOAD:

Evening

EVENING (DATE:)

THE 1 THING I DID TODAY THAT SCARED ME

TODAY I LEARNED/EXPERIENCED:

I AM PROUD OF MYSELF FOR:

THE THINGS I COULD WORK ON DOING BETTER ARE:

I AM BLESSED BECAUSE:

THOUGHT DOWNLOAD:

Morning

MORNING (DATE:)

TODAY, I AM THANKFUL FOR:
-
-
-
-
-

MY INTENTIONS/GOALS FOR TODAY ARE:
-
-
-

POSSIBLE OBSTACLES:

PREVENTATIVE/CONTINGENCY PLAN:

I WILL EMBODY "LOVE" BY: (SPECIFIC ACTIONS)

I FEEL EXCITED FOR/I FEEL APPREHENSIVE ABOUT:

THOUGHT DOWNLOAD:

Evening

EVENING (DATE:)

THE 1 THING I DID TODAY THAT SCARED ME

TODAY I LEARNED/EXPERIENCED:

I AM PROUD OF MYSELF FOR:

THE THINGS I COULD WORK ON DOING BETTER ARE:

I AM BLESSED BECAUSE:

THOUGHT DOWNLOAD:

Morning

MORNING (DATE:)

TODAY, I AM THANKFUL FOR:
-
-
-
-
-

MY INTENTIONS/GOALS FOR TODAY ARE:
-
-
-

POSSIBLE OBSTACLES:

PREVENTATIVE/CONTINGENCY PLAN:

I WILL EMBODY "LOVE" BY: (SPECIFIC ACTIONS)

I FEEL EXCITED FOR/I FEEL APPREHENSIVE ABOUT:

THOUGHT DOWNLOAD:

Evening

EVENING (DATE:)

THE 1 THING I DID TODAY THAT SCARED ME

TODAY I LEARNED/EXPERIENCED:

I AM PROUD OF MYSELF FOR:

THE THINGS I COULD WORK ON DOING BETTER ARE:

I AM BLESSED BECAUSE:

THOUGHT DOWNLOAD:

Morning

MORNING (DATE:)

MY INTENTIONS/GOALS FOR TODAY ARE:
-
-
-

TODAY, I AM THANKFUL FOR:
-
-
-
-
-

POSSIBLE OBSTACLES:

PREVENTATIVE/CONTINGENCY PLAN:

I WILL EMBODY "LOVE" BY: (SPECIFIC ACTIONS)

I FEEL EXCITED FOR/I FEEL APPREHENSIVE ABOUT:

THOUGHT DOWNLOAD:

Evening

EVENING (DATE:)

THE 1 THING I DID TODAY THAT SCARED ME

TODAY I LEARNED/EXPERIENCED:

I AM PROUD OF MYSELF FOR:

THE THINGS I COULD WORK ON DOING BETTER ARE:

I AM BLESSED BECAUSE:

THOUGHT DOWNLOAD:

Morning

MORNING (DATE:)

TODAY, I AM THANKFUL FOR:
-
-
-
-
-

MY INTENTIONS/GOALS FOR TODAY ARE:
-
-
-

POSSIBLE OBSTACLES:

PREVENTATIVE/CONTINGENCY PLAN:

I WILL EMBODY "LOVE" BY: (SPECIFIC ACTIONS)

I FEEL EXCITED FOR/I FEEL APPREHENSIVE ABOUT:

THOUGHT DOWNLOAD:

Evening

EVENING (DATE:)

THE 1 THING I DID TODAY THAT SCARED ME

TODAY I LEARNED/EXPERIENCED:

I AM PROUD OF MYSELF FOR:

THE THINGS I COULD WORK ON DOING BETTER ARE:

I AM BLESSED BECAUSE:

THOUGHT DOWNLOAD:

Morning

MORNING (DATE:)

MY INTENTIONS/GOALS FOR TODAY ARE:

-
-
-

TODAY, I AM THANKFUL FOR:

-
-
-
-
-

POSSIBLE OBSTACLES:

PREVENTATIVE/CONTINGENCY PLAN:

I WILL EMBODY "LOVE" BY: (SPECIFIC ACTIONS)

I FEEL EXCITED FOR/I FEEL APPREHENSIVE ABOUT:

THOUGHT DOWNLOAD:

Evening

EVENING (DATE:)

THE 1 THING I DID TODAY THAT SCARED ME

TODAY I LEARNED/EXPERIENCED:

I AM PROUD OF MYSELF FOR:

THE THINGS I COULD WORK ON DOING BETTER ARE:

I AM BLESSED BECAUSE:

THOUGHT DOWNLOAD:

Morning

MORNING (DATE:)

TODAY, I AM THANKFUL FOR:
-
-
-
-
-

MY INTENTIONS/GOALS FOR TODAY ARE:
-
-
-

POSSIBLE OBSTACLES:

PREVENTATIVE/CONTINGENCY PLAN:

I WILL EMBODY "LOVE" BY: (SPECIFIC ACTIONS)

I FEEL EXCITED FOR/I FEEL APPREHENSIVE ABOUT:

THOUGHT DOWNLOAD:

Evening

EVENING (DATE:)

THE 1 THING I DID TODAY THAT SCARED ME

TODAY I LEARNED/EXPERIENCED:

I AM PROUD OF MYSELF FOR:

THE THINGS I COULD WORK ON DOING BETTER ARE:

I AM BLESSED BECAUSE:

THOUGHT DOWNLOAD:

Morning

MORNING (DATE:)

MY INTENTIONS/GOALS FOR TODAY ARE:

-
-
-

TODAY, I AM THANKFUL FOR:

-
-
-
-
-

POSSIBLE OBSTACLES:

PREVENTATIVE/CONTINGENCY PLAN:

I WILL EMBODY "LOVE" BY: (SPECIFIC ACTIONS)

I FEEL EXCITED FOR/I FEEL APPREHENSIVE ABOUT:

THOUGHT DOWNLOAD:

Evening

EVENING (DATE:)

THE 1 THING I DID TODAY THAT SCARED ME

TODAY I LEARNED/EXPERIENCED:

I AM PROUD OF MYSELF FOR:

THE THINGS I COULD WORK ON DOING BETTER ARE:

I AM BLESSED BECAUSE:

THOUGHT DOWNLOAD:

Morning

MORNING (DATE:)

MY INTENTIONS/GOALS FOR TODAY ARE:
-
-
-

TODAY, I AM THANKFUL FOR:
-
-
-
-
-

POSSIBLE OBSTACLES:

PREVENTATIVE/CONTINGENCY PLAN:

I WILL EMBODY "LOVE" BY: (SPECIFIC ACTIONS)

I FEEL EXCITED FOR/I FEEL APPREHENSIVE ABOUT:

THOUGHT DOWNLOAD:

Evening

EVENING (DATE:)

THE 1 THING I DID TODAY THAT SCARED ME

TODAY I LEARNED/EXPERIENCED:

I AM PROUD OF MYSELF FOR:

THE THINGS I COULD WORK ON DOING BETTER ARE:

I AM BLESSED BECAUSE:

THOUGHT DOWNLOAD:

Morning

MORNING (DATE:)

MY INTENTIONS/GOALS FOR TODAY ARE:

-
-
-

TODAY, I AM THANKFUL FOR:

-
-
-
-
-

POSSIBLE OBSTACLES:

PREVENTATIVE/CONTINGENCY PLAN:

I WILL EMBODY "LOVE" BY: (SPECIFIC ACTIONS)

I FEEL EXCITED FOR/I FEEL APPREHENSIVE ABOUT:

THOUGHT DOWNLOAD:

Evening

EVENING (DATE:)

THE 1 THING I DID TODAY THAT SCARED ME

TODAY I LEARNED/EXPERIENCED:

I AM PROUD OF MYSELF FOR:

THE THINGS I COULD WORK ON DOING BETTER ARE:

I AM BLESSED BECAUSE:

THOUGHT DOWNLOAD:

Morning

MORNING (DATE:)

TODAY, I AM THANKFUL FOR:
-
-
-
-
-

MY INTENTIONS/GOALS FOR TODAY ARE:
-
-
-

POSSIBLE OBSTACLES:

PREVENTATIVE/CONTINGENCY PLAN:

I WILL EMBODY "LOVE" BY: (SPECIFIC ACTIONS)

I FEEL EXCITED FOR/I FEEL APPREHENSIVE ABOUT:

THOUGHT DOWNLOAD:

Evening

EVENING (DATE:)

THE 1 THING I DID TODAY THAT SCARED ME

TODAY I LEARNED/EXPERIENCED:

I AM PROUD OF MYSELF FOR:

THE THINGS I COULD WORK ON DOING BETTER ARE:

I AM BLESSED BECAUSE:

THOUGHT DOWNLOAD:

Morning

MORNING (DATE:)

MY INTENTIONS/GOALS FOR TODAY ARE:
-
-
-

TODAY, I AM THANKFUL FOR:
-
-
-
-
-

POSSIBLE OBSTACLES:

PREVENTATIVE/CONTINGENCY PLAN:

I WILL EMBODY "LOVE" BY: (SPECIFIC ACTIONS)

I FEEL EXCITED FOR/I FEEL APPREHENSIVE ABOUT:

THOUGHT DOWNLOAD:

Evening

EVENING (DATE:)

THE 1 THING I DID TODAY THAT SCARED ME

TODAY I LEARNED/EXPERIENCED:

I AM PROUD OF MYSELF FOR:

THE THINGS I COULD WORK ON DOING BETTER ARE:

I AM BLESSED BECAUSE:

THOUGHT DOWNLOAD:

Morning

MORNING (DATE:)

MY INTENTIONS/GOALS FOR TODAY ARE:
-
-
-

TODAY, I AM THANKFUL FOR:
-
-
-
-

POSSIBLE OBSTACLES:

PREVENTATIVE/CONTINGENCY PLAN:

I WILL EMBODY "LOVE" BY: (SPECIFIC ACTIONS)

I FEEL EXCITED FOR/I FEEL APPREHENSIVE ABOUT:

THOUGHT DOWNLOAD:

Evening

EVENING (DATE:)

THE 1 THING I DID TODAY THAT SCARED ME

TODAY I LEARNED/EXPERIENCED:

I AM PROUD OF MYSELF FOR:

THE THINGS I COULD WORK ON DOING BETTER ARE:

I AM BLESSED BECAUSE:

THOUGHT DOWNLOAD:

Morning

MORNING (DATE:)

MY INTENTIONS/GOALS FOR TODAY ARE:
-
-
-

TODAY, I AM THANKFUL FOR:
-
-
-
-
-

POSSIBLE OBSTACLES:

PREVENTATIVE/CONTINGENCY PLAN:

I WILL EMBODY "LOVE" BY: (SPECIFIC ACTIONS)

I FEEL EXCITED FOR/I FEEL APPREHENSIVE ABOUT:

THOUGHT DOWNLOAD:

Evening

EVENING (DATE:)

THE 1 THING I DID TODAY THAT SCARED ME

TODAY I LEARNED/EXPERIENCED:

I AM PROUD OF MYSELF FOR:

THE THINGS I COULD WORK ON DOING BETTER ARE:

I AM BLESSED BECAUSE:

THOUGHT DOWNLOAD:

Morning

MORNING (DATE:)

MY INTENTIONS/GOALS FOR TODAY ARE:
-
-
-

TODAY, I AM THANKFUL FOR:
-
-
-
-
-

POSSIBLE OBSTACLES:

PREVENTATIVE/CONTINGENCY PLAN:

I WILL EMBODY "LOVE" BY: (SPECIFIC ACTIONS)

I FEEL EXCITED FOR/I FEEL APPREHENSIVE ABOUT:

THOUGHT DOWNLOAD:

Evening

EVENING (DATE:)

THE 1 THING I DID TODAY THAT SCARED ME

TODAY I LEARNED/EXPERIENCED:

I AM PROUD OF MYSELF FOR:

THE THINGS I COULD WORK ON DOING BETTER ARE:

I AM BLESSED BECAUSE:

THOUGHT DOWNLOAD:

Morning

MORNING (DATE:)

MY INTENTIONS/GOALS FOR TODAY ARE:
-
-
-

TODAY, I AM THANKFUL FOR:
-
-
-
-
-

POSSIBLE OBSTACLES:

PREVENTATIVE/CONTINGENCY PLAN:

I WILL EMBODY "LOVE" BY: (SPECIFIC ACTIONS)

I FEEL EXCITED FOR/I FEEL APPREHENSIVE ABOUT:

THOUGHT DOWNLOAD:

Evening

EVENING (DATE:)

THE 1 THING I DID TODAY THAT SCARED ME

TODAY I LEARNED/EXPERIENCED:

I AM PROUD OF MYSELF FOR:

THE THINGS I COULD WORK ON DOING BETTER ARE:

I AM BLESSED BECAUSE:

THOUGHT DOWNLOAD:

Morning

MORNING (DATE:)

MY INTENTIONS/GOALS FOR TODAY ARE:
-
-
-

TODAY, I AM THANKFUL FOR:
-
-
-
-
-

POSSIBLE OBSTACLES:

PREVENTATIVE/CONTINGENCY PLAN:

I WILL EMBODY "LOVE" BY: (SPECIFIC ACTIONS)

I FEEL EXCITED FOR/I FEEL APPREHENSIVE ABOUT:

THOUGHT DOWNLOAD:

Evening

EVENING (DATE:)

THE 1 THING I DID TODAY THAT SCARED ME

TODAY I LEARNED/EXPERIENCED:

I AM PROUD OF MYSELF FOR:

THE THINGS I COULD WORK ON DOING BETTER ARE:

I AM BLESSED BECAUSE:

THOUGHT DOWNLOAD:

Morning

MORNING (DATE:)

MY INTENTIONS/GOALS FOR TODAY ARE:
-
-
-

TODAY, I AM THANKFUL FOR:
-
-
-
-
-

POSSIBLE OBSTACLES:

PREVENTATIVE/CONTINGENCY PLAN:

I WILL EMBODY "LOVE" BY: (SPECIFIC ACTIONS)

I FEEL EXCITED FOR/I FEEL APPREHENSIVE ABOUT:

THOUGHT DOWNLOAD:

Evening

EVENING (DATE:)

THE 1 THING I DID TODAY THAT SCARED ME

TODAY I LEARNED/EXPERIENCED:

I AM PROUD OF MYSELF FOR:

THE THINGS I COULD WORK ON DOING BETTER ARE:

I AM BLESSED BECAUSE:

THOUGHT DOWNLOAD:

Morning

MORNING (DATE:)

TODAY, I AM THANKFUL FOR:
-
-
-
-
-

MY INTENTIONS/GOALS FOR TODAY ARE:
-
-
-

POSSIBLE OBSTACLES:

PREVENTATIVE/CONTINGENCY PLAN:

I WILL EMBODY "LOVE" BY: (SPECIFIC ACTIONS)

I FEEL EXCITED FOR/I FEEL APPREHENSIVE ABOUT:

THOUGHT DOWNLOAD:

Evening

EVENING (DATE:)

THE 1 THING I DID TODAY THAT SCARED ME

TODAY I LEARNED/EXPERIENCED:

I AM PROUD OF MYSELF FOR:

THE THINGS I COULD WORK ON DOING BETTER ARE:

I AM BLESSED BECAUSE:

THOUGHT DOWNLOAD:

Morning

MORNING (DATE:)

TODAY, I AM THANKFUL FOR:
-
-
-
-
-

MY INTENTIONS/GOALS FOR TODAY ARE:
-
-
-

POSSIBLE OBSTACLES:

PREVENTATIVE/CONTINGENCY PLAN:

I WILL EMBODY "LOVE" BY: (SPECIFIC ACTIONS)

I FEEL EXCITED FOR/I FEEL APPREHENSIVE ABOUT:

THOUGHT DOWNLOAD:

Evening

EVENING (DATE:)

THE 1 THING I DID TODAY THAT SCARED ME

TODAY I LEARNED/EXPERIENCED:

I AM PROUD OF MYSELF FOR:

THE THINGS I COULD WORK ON DOING BETTER ARE:

I AM BLESSED BECAUSE:

THOUGHT DOWNLOAD:

Morning

MORNING (DATE:)

MY INTENTIONS/GOALS FOR TODAY ARE:

-
-
-

TODAY, I AM THANKFUL FOR:

-
-
-
-
-

POSSIBLE OBSTACLES:

PREVENTATIVE/CONTINGENCY PLAN:

I WILL EMBODY "LOVE" BY: (SPECIFIC ACTIONS)

I FEEL EXCITED FOR/I FEEL APPREHENSIVE ABOUT:

THOUGHT DOWNLOAD:

Evening

EVENING (DATE:)

THE 1 THING I DID TODAY THAT SCARED ME

TODAY I LEARNED/EXPERIENCED:

I AM PROUD OF MYSELF FOR:

THE THINGS I COULD WORK ON DOING BETTER ARE:

I AM BLESSED BECAUSE:

THOUGHT DOWNLOAD:

Morning

MORNING (DATE:)

MY INTENTIONS/GOALS FOR TODAY ARE:
-
-
-

TODAY, I AM THANKFUL FOR:
-
-
-
-
-

POSSIBLE OBSTACLES:

PREVENTATIVE/CONTINGENCY PLAN:

I WILL EMBODY "LOVE" BY: (SPECIFIC ACTIONS)

I FEEL EXCITED FOR/I FEEL APPREHENSIVE ABOUT:

THOUGHT DOWNLOAD:

Evening

EVENING (DATE:)

THE 1 THING I DID TODAY THAT SCARED ME

TODAY I LEARNED/EXPERIENCED:

I AM PROUD OF MYSELF FOR:

THE THINGS I COULD WORK ON DOING BETTER ARE:

I AM BLESSED BECAUSE:

THOUGHT DOWNLOAD:

Morning

MORNING (DATE:)

MY INTENTIONS/GOALS FOR TODAY ARE:
-
-
-

TODAY, I AM THANKFUL FOR:
-
-
-
-
-

POSSIBLE OBSTACLES:

PREVENTATIVE/CONTINGENCY PLAN:

I WILL EMBODY "LOVE" BY: (SPECIFIC ACTIONS)

I FEEL EXCITED FOR/I FEEL APPREHENSIVE ABOUT:

THOUGHT DOWNLOAD:

Evening

EVENING (DATE:)

THE 1 THING I DID TODAY THAT SCARED ME

TODAY I LEARNED/EXPERIENCED:

I AM PROUD OF MYSELF FOR:

THE THINGS I COULD WORK ON DOING BETTER ARE:

I AM BLESSED BECAUSE:

THOUGHT DOWNLOAD:

Morning

MORNING (DATE:)

MY INTENTIONS/GOALS FOR TODAY ARE:
-
-
-

TODAY, I AM THANKFUL FOR:
-
-
-
-
-

POSSIBLE OBSTACLES:

PREVENTATIVE/CONTINGENCY PLAN:

I WILL EMBODY "LOVE" BY: (SPECIFIC ACTIONS)

I FEEL EXCITED FOR/I FEEL APPREHENSIVE ABOUT:

THOUGHT DOWNLOAD:

Evening

EVENING (DATE:)

THE 1 THING I DID TODAY THAT SCARED ME

TODAY I LEARNED/EXPERIENCED:

I AM PROUD OF MYSELF FOR:

THE THINGS I COULD WORK ON DOING BETTER ARE:

I AM BLESSED BECAUSE:

THOUGHT DOWNLOAD:

Morning

MORNING (DATE:)

MY INTENTIONS/GOALS FOR TODAY ARE:

-
-
-

TODAY, I AM THANKFUL FOR:

-
-
-
-
-

POSSIBLE OBSTACLES:

PREVENTATIVE/CONTINGENCY PLAN:

I WILL EMBODY "LOVE" BY: (SPECIFIC ACTIONS)

I FEEL EXCITED FOR/I FEEL APPREHENSIVE ABOUT:

THOUGHT DOWNLOAD:

Evening

EVENING (DATE:)

THE 1 THING I DID TODAY THAT SCARED ME

TODAY I LEARNED/EXPERIENCED:

I AM PROUD OF MYSELF FOR:

THE THINGS I COULD WORK ON DOING BETTER ARE:

I AM BLESSED BECAUSE:

THOUGHT DOWNLOAD:

Morning

MORNING (DATE:)

MY INTENTIONS/GOALS FOR TODAY ARE:
-
-
-

TODAY, I AM THANKFUL FOR:
-
-
-
-
-

POSSIBLE OBSTACLES:

PREVENTATIVE/CONTINGENCY PLAN:

I WILL EMBODY "LOVE" BY: (SPECIFIC ACTIONS)

I FEEL EXCITED FOR/I FEEL APPREHENSIVE ABOUT:

THOUGHT DOWNLOAD:

Evening

EVENING (DATE:)

THE 1 THING I DID TODAY THAT SCARED ME

TODAY I LEARNED/EXPERIENCED:

I AM PROUD OF MYSELF FOR:

THE THINGS I COULD WORK ON DOING BETTER ARE:

I AM BLESSED BECAUSE:

THOUGHT DOWNLOAD:

Morning

MORNING (DATE:)

TODAY, I AM THANKFUL FOR:
-
-
-
-
-

MY INTENTIONS/GOALS FOR TODAY ARE:
-
-
-

POSSIBLE OBSTACLES:

PREVENTATIVE/CONTINGENCY PLAN:

I WILL EMBODY "LOVE" BY: (SPECIFIC ACTIONS)

I FEEL EXCITED FOR/I FEEL APPREHENSIVE ABOUT:

THOUGHT DOWNLOAD:

Evening

EVENING (DATE:)

THE 1 THING I DID TODAY THAT SCARED ME

TODAY I LEARNED/EXPERIENCED:

I AM PROUD OF MYSELF FOR:

THE THINGS I COULD WORK ON DOING BETTER ARE:

I AM BLESSED BECAUSE:

THOUGHT DOWNLOAD:

Morning

MORNING (DATE:)

MY INTENTIONS/GOALS FOR TODAY ARE:
-
-
-

TODAY, I AM THANKFUL FOR:
-
-
-
-

POSSIBLE OBSTACLES:

PREVENTATIVE/CONTINGENCY PLAN:

I WILL EMBODY "LOVE" BY: (SPECIFIC ACTIONS)

I FEEL EXCITED FOR/I FEEL APPREHENSIVE ABOUT:

THOUGHT DOWNLOAD:

Evening

EVENING (DATE:)

THE 1 THING I DID TODAY THAT SCARED ME

TODAY I LEARNED/EXPERIENCED:

I AM PROUD OF MYSELF FOR:

THE THINGS I COULD WORK ON DOING BETTER ARE:

I AM BLESSED BECAUSE:

THOUGHT DOWNLOAD:

Morning

MORNING (DATE:)

MY INTENTIONS/GOALS FOR TODAY ARE:
-
-
-

TODAY, I AM THANKFUL FOR:
-
-
-
-
-

POSSIBLE OBSTACLES:

PREVENTATIVE/CONTINGENCY PLAN:

I WILL EMBODY "LOVE" BY: (SPECIFIC ACTIONS)

I FEEL EXCITED FOR/I FEEL APPREHENSIVE ABOUT:

THOUGHT DOWNLOAD:

Evening

EVENING (DATE:)

THE 1 THING I DID TODAY THAT SCARED ME

TODAY I LEARNED/EXPERIENCED:

I AM PROUD OF MYSELF FOR:

THE THINGS I COULD WORK ON DOING BETTER ARE:

I AM BLESSED BECAUSE:

THOUGHT DOWNLOAD:

Morning

MORNING (DATE:)

MY INTENTIONS/GOALS FOR TODAY ARE:
-
-
-

TODAY, I AM THANKFUL FOR:
-
-
-
-
-

POSSIBLE OBSTACLES:

PREVENTATIVE/CONTINGENCY PLAN:

I WILL EMBODY "LOVE" BY: (SPECIFIC ACTIONS)

I FEEL EXCITED FOR/I FEEL APPREHENSIVE ABOUT:

THOUGHT DOWNLOAD:

Evening

EVENING (DATE:)

THE 1 THING I DID TODAY THAT SCARED ME

TODAY I LEARNED/EXPERIENCED:

I AM PROUD OF MYSELF FOR:

THE THINGS I COULD WORK ON DOING BETTER ARE:

I AM BLESSED BECAUSE:

THOUGHT DOWNLOAD:

Morning

MORNING (DATE:)

MY INTENTIONS/GOALS FOR TODAY ARE:
-
-
-

TODAY, I AM THANKFUL FOR:
-
-
-
-
-

POSSIBLE OBSTACLES:

PREVENTATIVE/CONTINGENCY PLAN:

I WILL EMBODY "LOVE" BY: (SPECIFIC ACTIONS)

I FEEL EXCITED FOR/I FEEL APPREHENSIVE ABOUT:

THOUGHT DOWNLOAD:

Evening

EVENING (DATE:)

THE 1 THING I DID TODAY THAT SCARED ME

TODAY I LEARNED/EXPERIENCED:

I AM PROUD OF MYSELF FOR:

THE THINGS I COULD WORK ON DOING BETTER ARE:

I AM BLESSED BECAUSE:

THOUGHT DOWNLOAD:

Morning

MORNING (DATE:)

TODAY, I AM THANKFUL FOR:
-
-
-
-
-

MY INTENTIONS/GOALS FOR TODAY ARE:
-
-
-

POSSIBLE OBSTACLES:

PREVENTATIVE/CONTINGENCY PLAN:

I WILL EMBODY "LOVE" BY: (SPECIFIC ACTIONS)

I FEEL EXCITED FOR/I FEEL APPREHENSIVE ABOUT:

THOUGHT DOWNLOAD:

Evening

EVENING (DATE:)

THE 1 THING I DID TODAY THAT SCARED ME

TODAY I LEARNED/EXPERIENCED:

I AM PROUD OF MYSELF FOR:

THE THINGS I COULD WORK ON DOING BETTER ARE:

I AM BLESSED BECAUSE:

THOUGHT DOWNLOAD:

Morning

MORNING (DATE:)

MY INTENTIONS/GOALS FOR TODAY ARE:
-
-
-

TODAY, I AM THANKFUL FOR:
-
-
-
-
-

POSSIBLE OBSTACLES:

PREVENTATIVE/CONTINGENCY PLAN:

I WILL EMBODY "LOVE" BY: (SPECIFIC ACTIONS)

I FEEL EXCITED FOR/I FEEL APPREHENSIVE ABOUT:

THOUGHT DOWNLOAD:

Evening

EVENING (DATE:)

THE 1 THING I DID TODAY THAT SCARED ME

TODAY I LEARNED/EXPERIENCED:

I AM PROUD OF MYSELF FOR:

THE THINGS I COULD WORK ON DOING BETTER ARE:

I AM BLESSED BECAUSE:

THOUGHT DOWNLOAD:

Morning

MORNING (DATE:)

TODAY, I AM THANKFUL FOR:

-
-
-
-
-

MY INTENTIONS/GOALS FOR TODAY ARE:

-
-
-

POSSIBLE OBSTACLES:

PREVENTATIVE/CONTINGENCY PLAN:

I WILL EMBODY "LOVE" BY: (SPECIFIC ACTIONS)

I FEEL EXCITED FOR/I FEEL APPREHENSIVE ABOUT:

THOUGHT DOWNLOAD:

Evening

EVENING (DATE:)

THE 1 THING I DID TODAY THAT SCARED ME

TODAY I LEARNED/EXPERIENCED:

I AM PROUD OF MYSELF FOR:

THE THINGS I COULD WORK ON DOING BETTER ARE:

I AM BLESSED BECAUSE:

THOUGHT DOWNLOAD:

Morning

MORNING (DATE:)

MY INTENTIONS/GOALS FOR TODAY ARE:

-
-
-

TODAY, I AM THANKFUL FOR:

-
-
-
-
-

POSSIBLE OBSTACLES:

PREVENTATIVE/CONTINGENCY PLAN:

I WILL EMBODY "LOVE" BY: (SPECIFIC ACTIONS)

I FEEL EXCITED FOR/I FEEL APPREHENSIVE ABOUT:

THOUGHT DOWNLOAD:

Evening

EVENING (DATE:)

THE 1 THING I DID TODAY THAT SCARED ME

TODAY I LEARNED/EXPERIENCED:

I AM PROUD OF MYSELF FOR:

THE THINGS I COULD WORK ON DOING BETTER ARE:

I AM BLESSED BECAUSE:

THOUGHT DOWNLOAD:

Morning

MORNING (DATE:)

MY INTENTIONS/GOALS FOR TODAY ARE:

-
-
-

TODAY, I AM THANKFUL FOR:

-
-
-
-

POSSIBLE OBSTACLES:

PREVENTATIVE/CONTINGENCY PLAN:

I WILL EMBODY "LOVE" BY: (SPECIFIC ACTIONS)

I FEEL EXCITED FOR/I FEEL APPREHENSIVE ABOUT:

THOUGHT DOWNLOAD:

Evening

EVENING (DATE:)

THE 1 THING I DID TODAY THAT SCARED ME

TODAY I LEARNED/EXPERIENCED:

I AM PROUD OF MYSELF FOR:

THE THINGS I COULD WORK ON DOING BETTER ARE:

I AM BLESSED BECAUSE:

THOUGHT DOWNLOAD:

Morning

MORNING (DATE:)

MY INTENTIONS/GOALS FOR TODAY ARE:
-
-
-

TODAY, I AM THANKFUL FOR:
-
-
-
-
-

POSSIBLE OBSTACLES:

PREVENTATIVE/CONTINGENCY PLAN:

I WILL EMBODY "LOVE" BY: (SPECIFIC ACTIONS)

I FEEL EXCITED FOR/I FEEL APPREHENSIVE ABOUT:

THOUGHT DOWNLOAD:

Evening

EVENING (DATE:)

THE 1 THING I DID TODAY THAT SCARED ME

TODAY I LEARNED/EXPERIENCED:

I AM PROUD OF MYSELF FOR:

THE THINGS I COULD WORK ON DOING BETTER ARE:

I AM BLESSED BECAUSE:

THOUGHT DOWNLOAD:

Morning

MORNING (DATE:)

MY INTENTIONS/GOALS FOR TODAY ARE:
-
-
-

TODAY, I AM THANKFUL FOR:
-
-
-
-

POSSIBLE OBSTACLES:

PREVENTATIVE/CONTINGENCY PLAN:

I WILL EMBODY "LOVE" BY: (SPECIFIC ACTIONS)

I FEEL EXCITED FOR/I FEEL APPREHENSIVE ABOUT:

THOUGHT DOWNLOAD:

Evening

EVENING (DATE:)

THE 1 THING I DID TODAY THAT SCARED ME

TODAY I LEARNED/EXPERIENCED:

I AM PROUD OF MYSELF FOR:

THE THINGS I COULD WORK ON DOING BETTER ARE:

I AM BLESSED BECAUSE:

THOUGHT DOWNLOAD:

Morning

MORNING (DATE:)

MY INTENTIONS/GOALS FOR TODAY ARE:

-
-
-

TODAY, I AM THANKFUL FOR:

-
-
-
-
-

POSSIBLE OBSTACLES:

PREVENTATIVE/CONTINGENCY PLAN:

I WILL EMBODY "LOVE" BY: (SPECIFIC ACTIONS)

I FEEL EXCITED FOR/I FEEL APPREHENSIVE ABOUT:

THOUGHT DOWNLOAD:

Evening

EVENING (DATE:)

THE 1 THING I DID TODAY THAT SCARED ME

TODAY I LEARNED/EXPERIENCED:

I AM PROUD OF MYSELF FOR:

THE THINGS I COULD WORK ON DOING BETTER ARE:

I AM BLESSED BECAUSE:

THOUGHT DOWNLOAD:

Morning

MORNING (DATE:)

MY INTENTIONS/GOALS FOR TODAY ARE:

-
-
-

TODAY, I AM THANKFUL FOR:

-
-
-
-
-

POSSIBLE OBSTACLES:

PREVENTATIVE/CONTINGENCY PLAN:

I WILL EMBODY "LOVE" BY: (SPECIFIC ACTIONS)

I FEEL EXCITED FOR/I FEEL APPREHENSIVE ABOUT:

THOUGHT DOWNLOAD:

Evening

EVENING (DATE:)

THE 1 THING I DID TODAY THAT SCARED ME

TODAY I LEARNED/EXPERIENCED:

I AM PROUD OF MYSELF FOR:

THE THINGS I COULD WORK ON DOING BETTER ARE:

I AM BLESSED BECAUSE:

THOUGHT DOWNLOAD:

Morning

MORNING (DATE:)

MY INTENTIONS/GOALS FOR TODAY ARE:

-
-
-

TODAY, I AM THANKFUL FOR:

-
-
-
-
-

POSSIBLE OBSTACLES:

PREVENTATIVE/CONTINGENCY PLAN:

I WILL EMBODY "LOVE" BY: (SPECIFIC ACTIONS)

I FEEL EXCITED FOR/I FEEL APPREHENSIVE ABOUT:

THOUGHT DOWNLOAD:

Evening

EVENING (DATE:)

THE 1 THING I DID TODAY THAT SCARED ME

TODAY I LEARNED/EXPERIENCED:

I AM PROUD OF MYSELF FOR:

THE THINGS I COULD WORK ON DOING BETTER ARE:

I AM BLESSED BECAUSE:

THOUGHT DOWNLOAD:

Morning

MORNING (DATE:)

MY INTENTIONS/GOALS FOR TODAY ARE:
-
-
-

TODAY, I AM THANKFUL FOR:
-
-
-
-
-

POSSIBLE OBSTACLES:

PREVENTATIVE/CONTINGENCY PLAN:

I WILL EMBODY "LOVE" BY: (SPECIFIC ACTIONS)

I FEEL EXCITED FOR/I FEEL APPREHENSIVE ABOUT:

THOUGHT DOWNLOAD:

Evening

EVENING (DATE:)

THE 1 THING I DID TODAY THAT SCARED ME

TODAY I LEARNED/EXPERIENCED:

I AM PROUD OF MYSELF FOR:

THE THINGS I COULD WORK ON DOING BETTER ARE:

I AM BLESSED BECAUSE:

THOUGHT DOWNLOAD:

Morning

MORNING (DATE:)

MY INTENTIONS/GOALS FOR TODAY ARE:

-
-
-

TODAY, I AM THANKFUL FOR:

-
-
-
-

POSSIBLE OBSTACLES:

PREVENTATIVE/CONTINGENCY PLAN:

I WILL EMBODY "LOVE" BY: (SPECIFIC ACTIONS)

I FEEL EXCITED FOR/I FEEL APPREHENSIVE ABOUT:

THOUGHT DOWNLOAD:

Evening

EVENING (DATE:)

THE 1 THING I DID TODAY THAT SCARED ME

TODAY I LEARNED/EXPERIENCED:

I AM PROUD OF MYSELF FOR:

THE THINGS I COULD WORK ON DOING BETTER ARE:

I AM BLESSED BECAUSE:

THOUGHT DOWNLOAD:

Morning

MORNING (DATE:)

MY INTENTIONS/GOALS FOR TODAY ARE:

-
-
-

TODAY, I AM THANKFUL FOR:

-
-
-
-
-

POSSIBLE OBSTACLES:

PREVENTATIVE/CONTINGENCY PLAN:

I WILL EMBODY "LOVE" BY: (SPECIFIC ACTIONS)

I FEEL EXCITED FOR/I FEEL APPREHENSIVE ABOUT:

THOUGHT DOWNLOAD:

Evening

EVENING (DATE:)

THE 1 THING I DID TODAY THAT SCARED ME

TODAY I LEARNED/EXPERIENCED:

I AM PROUD OF MYSELF FOR:

THE THINGS I COULD WORK ON DOING BETTER ARE:

I AM BLESSED BECAUSE:

THOUGHT DOWNLOAD:

Morning

MORNING (DATE:)

TODAY, I AM THANKFUL FOR:
-
-
-
-
-

MY INTENTIONS/GOALS FOR TODAY ARE:
-
-
-

POSSIBLE OBSTACLES:

PREVENTATIVE/CONTINGENCY PLAN:

I WILL EMBODY "LOVE" BY: (SPECIFIC ACTIONS)

I FEEL EXCITED FOR/I FEEL APPREHENSIVE ABOUT:

THOUGHT DOWNLOAD:

Evening

EVENING (DATE:)

THE 1 THING I DID TODAY THAT SCARED ME

TODAY I LEARNED/EXPERIENCED:

I AM PROUD OF MYSELF FOR:

THE THINGS I COULD WORK ON DOING BETTER ARE:

I AM BLESSED BECAUSE:

THOUGHT DOWNLOAD:

Morning

MORNING (DATE:)

MY INTENTIONS/GOALS FOR TODAY ARE:
-
-
-

TODAY, I AM THANKFUL FOR:
-
-
-
-
-

POSSIBLE OBSTACLES:

PREVENTATIVE/CONTINGENCY PLAN:

I WILL EMBODY "LOVE" BY: (SPECIFIC ACTIONS)

I FEEL EXCITED FOR/I FEEL APPREHENSIVE ABOUT:

THOUGHT DOWNLOAD:

Evening

EVENING (DATE:)

THE 1 THING I DID TODAY THAT SCARED ME

TODAY I LEARNED/EXPERIENCED:

I AM PROUD OF MYSELF FOR:

THE THINGS I COULD WORK ON DOING BETTER ARE:

I AM BLESSED BECAUSE:

THOUGHT DOWNLOAD:

Morning

MORNING (DATE:)

MY INTENTIONS/GOALS FOR TODAY ARE:

-
-
-

TODAY, I AM THANKFUL FOR:

-
-
-
-
-

POSSIBLE OBSTACLES:

PREVENTATIVE/CONTINGENCY PLAN:

I WILL EMBODY "LOVE" BY: (SPECIFIC ACTIONS)

I FEEL EXCITED FOR/I FEEL APPREHENSIVE ABOUT:

THOUGHT DOWNLOAD:

Evening

EVENING (DATE:)

THE 1 THING I DID TODAY THAT SCARED ME

TODAY I LEARNED/EXPERIENCED:

I AM PROUD OF MYSELF FOR:

THE THINGS I COULD WORK ON DOING BETTER ARE:

I AM BLESSED BECAUSE:

THOUGHT DOWNLOAD:

Morning

MORNING (DATE:)

MY INTENTIONS/GOALS FOR TODAY ARE:
-
-
-

TODAY, I AM THANKFUL FOR:
-
-
-
-
-

POSSIBLE OBSTACLES:

PREVENTATIVE/CONTINGENCY PLAN:

I WILL EMBODY "LOVE" BY: (SPECIFIC ACTIONS)

I FEEL EXCITED FOR/I FEEL APPREHENSIVE ABOUT:

THOUGHT DOWNLOAD:

Evening

EVENING (DATE:)

THE 1 THING I DID TODAY THAT SCARED ME

TODAY I LEARNED/EXPERIENCED:

I AM PROUD OF MYSELF FOR:

THE THINGS I COULD WORK ON DOING BETTER ARE:

I AM BLESSED BECAUSE:

THOUGHT DOWNLOAD:

Morning

MORNING (DATE:)

MY INTENTIONS/GOALS FOR TODAY ARE:
-
-
-

TODAY, I AM THANKFUL FOR:
-
-
-
-
-

POSSIBLE OBSTACLES:

PREVENTATIVE/CONTINGENCY PLAN:

I WILL EMBODY "LOVE" BY: (SPECIFIC ACTIONS)

I FEEL EXCITED FOR/I FEEL APPREHENSIVE ABOUT:

THOUGHT DOWNLOAD:

Evening

EVENING (DATE:)

THE 1 THING I DID TODAY THAT SCARED ME

TODAY I LEARNED/EXPERIENCED:

I AM PROUD OF MYSELF FOR:

THE THINGS I COULD WORK ON DOING BETTER ARE:

I AM BLESSED BECAUSE:

THOUGHT DOWNLOAD:

Morning

MORNING (DATE:)

MY INTENTIONS/GOALS FOR TODAY ARE:
-
-
-

TODAY, I AM THANKFUL FOR:
-
-
-
-
-

POSSIBLE OBSTACLES:

PREVENTATIVE/CONTINGENCY PLAN:

I WILL EMBODY "LOVE" BY: (SPECIFIC ACTIONS)

I FEEL EXCITED FOR/I FEEL APPREHENSIVE ABOUT:

THOUGHT DOWNLOAD:

Evening

EVENING (DATE:)

THE 1 THING I DID TODAY THAT SCARED ME

TODAY I LEARNED/EXPERIENCED:

I AM PROUD OF MYSELF FOR:

THE THINGS I COULD WORK ON DOING BETTER ARE:

I AM BLESSED BECAUSE:

THOUGHT DOWNLOAD:

Morning

MORNING (DATE:)

MY INTENTIONS/GOALS FOR TODAY ARE:
-
-
-

TODAY, I AM THANKFUL FOR:
-
-
-
-
-

POSSIBLE OBSTACLES:

PREVENTATIVE/CONTINGENCY PLAN:

I WILL EMBODY "LOVE" BY: (SPECIFIC ACTIONS)

I FEEL EXCITED FOR/I FEEL APPREHENSIVE ABOUT:

THOUGHT DOWNLOAD:

Evening

EVENING (DATE:)

THE 1 THING I DID TODAY THAT SCARED ME

TODAY I LEARNED/EXPERIENCED:

I AM PROUD OF MYSELF FOR:

THE THINGS I COULD WORK ON DOING BETTER ARE:

I AM BLESSED BECAUSE:

THOUGHT DOWNLOAD:

Morning

MORNING (DATE:)

MY INTENTIONS/GOALS FOR TODAY ARE:
-
-
-

TODAY, I AM THANKFUL FOR:
-
-
-
-
-

POSSIBLE OBSTACLES:

PREVENTATIVE/CONTINGENCY PLAN:

I WILL EMBODY "LOVE" BY: (SPECIFIC ACTIONS)

I FEEL EXCITED FOR/I FEEL APPREHENSIVE ABOUT:

THOUGHT DOWNLOAD:

Evening

EVENING (DATE:)

THE 1 THING I DID TODAY THAT SCARED ME

TODAY I LEARNED/EXPERIENCED:

I AM PROUD OF MYSELF FOR:

THE THINGS I COULD WORK ON DOING BETTER ARE:

I AM BLESSED BECAUSE:

THOUGHT DOWNLOAD:

Morning

MORNING (DATE:)

MY INTENTIONS/GOALS FOR TODAY ARE:
-
-
-

TODAY, I AM THANKFUL FOR:
-
-
-
-
-

POSSIBLE OBSTACLES:

PREVENTATIVE/CONTINGENCY PLAN:

I WILL EMBODY "LOVE" BY: (SPECIFIC ACTIONS)

I FEEL EXCITED FOR/I FEEL APPREHENSIVE ABOUT:

THOUGHT DOWNLOAD:

Evening

EVENING (DATE:)

THE 1 THING I DID TODAY THAT SCARED ME

TODAY I LEARNED/EXPERIENCED:

I AM PROUD OF MYSELF FOR:

THE THINGS I COULD WORK ON DOING BETTER ARE:

I AM BLESSED BECAUSE:

THOUGHT DOWNLOAD:

Morning

MORNING (DATE:)

MY INTENTIONS/GOALS FOR TODAY ARE:

-
-
-

TODAY, I AM THANKFUL FOR:

-
-
-
-
-

POSSIBLE OBSTACLES:

PREVENTATIVE/CONTINGENCY PLAN:

I WILL EMBODY "LOVE" BY: (SPECIFIC ACTIONS)

I FEEL EXCITED FOR/I FEEL APPREHENSIVE ABOUT:

THOUGHT DOWNLOAD:

Evening

EVENING (DATE:)

THE 1 THING I DID TODAY THAT SCARED ME

TODAY I LEARNED/EXPERIENCED:

I AM PROUD OF MYSELF FOR:

THE THINGS I COULD WORK ON DOING BETTER ARE:

I AM BLESSED BECAUSE:

THOUGHT DOWNLOAD:

Morning

MORNING (DATE:)

MY INTENTIONS/GOALS FOR TODAY ARE:

-
-
-

TODAY, I AM THANKFUL FOR:

-
-
-
-

POSSIBLE OBSTACLES:

PREVENTATIVE/CONTINGENCY PLAN:

I WILL EMBODY "LOVE" BY: (SPECIFIC ACTIONS)

I FEEL EXCITED FOR/I FEEL APPREHENSIVE ABOUT:

THOUGHT DOWNLOAD:

Evening

EVENING (DATE:)

THE 1 THING I DID TODAY THAT SCARED ME

TODAY I LEARNED/EXPERIENCED:

I AM PROUD OF MYSELF FOR:

THE THINGS I COULD WORK ON DOING BETTER ARE:

I AM BLESSED BECAUSE:

THOUGHT DOWNLOAD:

Morning

MORNING (DATE:)

MY INTENTIONS/GOALS FOR TODAY ARE:

-
-
-

TODAY, I AM THANKFUL FOR:

-
-
-
-
-

POSSIBLE OBSTACLES:

PREVENTATIVE/CONTINGENCY PLAN:

I WILL EMBODY "LOVE" BY: (SPECIFIC ACTIONS)

I FEEL EXCITED FOR/I FEEL APPREHENSIVE ABOUT:

THOUGHT DOWNLOAD:

Evening

EVENING (DATE:)

THE 1 THING I DID TODAY THAT SCARED ME

TODAY I LEARNED/EXPERIENCED:

I AM PROUD OF MYSELF FOR:

THE THINGS I COULD WORK ON DOING BETTER ARE:

I AM BLESSED BECAUSE:

THOUGHT DOWNLOAD:

Morning

MORNING (DATE:)

MY INTENTIONS/GOALS FOR TODAY ARE:
-
-
-

TODAY, I AM THANKFUL FOR:
-
-
-
-
-

POSSIBLE OBSTACLES:

PREVENTATIVE/CONTINGENCY PLAN:

I WILL EMBODY "LOVE" BY: (SPECIFIC ACTIONS)

I FEEL EXCITED FOR/I FEEL APPREHENSIVE ABOUT:

THOUGHT DOWNLOAD:

Evening

EVENING (DATE:)

THE 1 THING I DID TODAY THAT SCARED ME

TODAY I LEARNED/EXPERIENCED:

I AM PROUD OF MYSELF FOR:

THE THINGS I COULD WORK ON DOING BETTER ARE:

I AM BLESSED BECAUSE:

THOUGHT DOWNLOAD:

Morning

MORNING (DATE:)

MY INTENTIONS/GOALS FOR TODAY ARE:

-
-
-

TODAY, I AM THANKFUL FOR:

-
-
-
-
-

POSSIBLE OBSTACLES:

PREVENTATIVE/CONTINGENCY PLAN:

I WILL EMBODY "LOVE" BY: (SPECIFIC ACTIONS)

I FEEL EXCITED FOR/I FEEL APPREHENSIVE ABOUT:

THOUGHT DOWNLOAD:

Evening

EVENING (DATE:)

THE 1 THING I DID TODAY THAT SCARED ME

TODAY I LEARNED/EXPERIENCED:

I AM PROUD OF MYSELF FOR:

THE THINGS I COULD WORK ON DOING BETTER ARE:

I AM BLESSED BECAUSE:

THOUGHT DOWNLOAD:

Morning

MORNING (DATE:)

MY INTENTIONS/GOALS FOR TODAY ARE:
-
-
-

TODAY, I AM THANKFUL FOR:
-
-
-
-
-

POSSIBLE OBSTACLES:

PREVENTATIVE/CONTINGENCY PLAN:

I WILL EMBODY "LOVE" BY: (SPECIFIC ACTIONS)

I FEEL EXCITED FOR/I FEEL APPREHENSIVE ABOUT:

THOUGHT DOWNLOAD:

Evening

EVENING (DATE:)

THE 1 THING I DID TODAY THAT SCARED ME

TODAY I LEARNED/EXPERIENCED:

I AM PROUD OF MYSELF FOR:

THE THINGS I COULD WORK ON DOING BETTER ARE:

I AM BLESSED BECAUSE:

THOUGHT DOWNLOAD:

Morning

MORNING (DATE:)

MY INTENTIONS/GOALS FOR TODAY ARE:
-
-
-

TODAY, I AM THANKFUL FOR:
-
-
-
-
-

POSSIBLE OBSTACLES:

PREVENTATIVE/CONTINGENCY PLAN:

I WILL EMBODY "LOVE" BY: (SPECIFIC ACTIONS)

I FEEL EXCITED FOR/I FEEL APPREHENSIVE ABOUT:

THOUGHT DOWNLOAD:

Evening

EVENING (DATE:)

THE 1 THING I DID TODAY THAT SCARED ME

TODAY I LEARNED/EXPERIENCED:

I AM PROUD OF MYSELF FOR:

THE THINGS I COULD WORK ON DOING BETTER ARE:

I AM BLESSED BECAUSE:

THOUGHT DOWNLOAD:

Morning

MORNING (DATE:)

MY INTENTIONS/GOALS FOR TODAY ARE:
-
-
-

TODAY, I AM THANKFUL FOR:
-
-
-
-
-

POSSIBLE OBSTACLES:

PREVENTATIVE/CONTINGENCY PLAN:

I WILL EMBODY "LOVE" BY: (SPECIFIC ACTIONS)

I FEEL EXCITED FOR/I FEEL APPREHENSIVE ABOUT:

THOUGHT DOWNLOAD:

Evening

EVENING (DATE:)

THE 1 THING I DID TODAY THAT SCARED ME

TODAY I LEARNED/EXPERIENCED:

I AM PROUD OF MYSELF FOR:

THE THINGS I COULD WORK ON DOING BETTER ARE:

I AM BLESSED BECAUSE:

THOUGHT DOWNLOAD:

Morning

MORNING (DATE:)

MY INTENTIONS/GOALS FOR TODAY ARE:
-
-
-

TODAY, I AM THANKFUL FOR:
-
-
-
-
-

POSSIBLE OBSTACLES:

PREVENTATIVE/CONTINGENCY PLAN:

I WILL EMBODY "LOVE" BY: (SPECIFIC ACTIONS)

I FEEL EXCITED FOR/I FEEL APPREHENSIVE ABOUT:

THOUGHT DOWNLOAD:

Evening

EVENING (DATE:)

THE 1 THING I DID TODAY THAT SCARED ME

TODAY I LEARNED/EXPERIENCED:

I AM PROUD OF MYSELF FOR:

THE THINGS I COULD WORK ON DOING BETTER ARE:

I AM BLESSED BECAUSE:

THOUGHT DOWNLOAD:

Morning

MORNING (DATE:)

MY INTENTIONS/GOALS FOR TODAY ARE:
-
-
-

TODAY, I AM THANKFUL FOR:
-
-
-
-
-

POSSIBLE OBSTACLES:

PREVENTATIVE/CONTINGENCY PLAN:

I WILL EMBODY "LOVE" BY: (SPECIFIC ACTIONS)

I FEEL EXCITED FOR/I FEEL APPREHENSIVE ABOUT:

THOUGHT DOWNLOAD:

Evening

EVENING (DATE:)

THE 1 THING I DID TODAY THAT SCARED ME

TODAY I LEARNED/EXPERIENCED:

I AM PROUD OF MYSELF FOR:

THE THINGS I COULD WORK ON DOING BETTER ARE:

I AM BLESSED BECAUSE:

THOUGHT DOWNLOAD:

Morning

MORNING (DATE:)

MY INTENTIONS/GOALS FOR TODAY ARE:
-
-
-

TODAY, I AM THANKFUL FOR:
-
-
-
-
-

POSSIBLE OBSTACLES:

PREVENTATIVE/CONTINGENCY PLAN:

I WILL EMBODY "LOVE" BY: (SPECIFIC ACTIONS)

I FEEL EXCITED FOR/I FEEL APPREHENSIVE ABOUT:

THOUGHT DOWNLOAD:

Evening

EVENING (DATE:)

THE 1 THING I DID TODAY THAT SCARED ME

TODAY I LEARNED/EXPERIENCED:

I AM PROUD OF MYSELF FOR:

THE THINGS I COULD WORK ON DOING BETTER ARE:

I AM BLESSED BECAUSE:

THOUGHT DOWNLOAD:

Morning

MORNING (DATE:)

MY INTENTIONS/GOALS FOR TODAY ARE:

-
-
-

TODAY, I AM THANKFUL FOR:

-
-
-
-

POSSIBLE OBSTACLES:

PREVENTATIVE/CONTINGENCY PLAN:

I WILL EMBODY "LOVE" BY: (SPECIFIC ACTIONS)

I FEEL EXCITED FOR/I FEEL APPREHENSIVE ABOUT:

THOUGHT DOWNLOAD:

Evening

EVENING (DATE:)

THE 1 THING I DID TODAY THAT SCARED ME

TODAY I LEARNED/EXPERIENCED:

I AM PROUD OF MYSELF FOR:

THE THINGS I COULD WORK ON DOING BETTER ARE:

I AM BLESSED BECAUSE:

THOUGHT DOWNLOAD:

Morning

MORNING (DATE:)

MY INTENTIONS/GOALS FOR TODAY ARE:

-
-
-

TODAY, I AM THANKFUL FOR:

-
-
-
-
-

POSSIBLE OBSTACLES:

PREVENTATIVE/CONTINGENCY PLAN:

I WILL EMBODY "LOVE" BY: (SPECIFIC ACTIONS)

I FEEL EXCITED FOR/I FEEL APPREHENSIVE ABOUT:

THOUGHT DOWNLOAD:

Evening

EVENING (DATE:)

THE 1 THING I DID TODAY THAT SCARED ME

TODAY I LEARNED/EXPERIENCED:

I AM PROUD OF MYSELF FOR:

THE THINGS I COULD WORK ON DOING BETTER ARE:

I AM BLESSED BECAUSE:

THOUGHT DOWNLOAD:

Morning

MORNING (DATE:)

MY INTENTIONS/GOALS FOR TODAY ARE:

-
-
-

TODAY, I AM THANKFUL FOR:

-
-
-
-
-

POSSIBLE OBSTACLES:

PREVENTATIVE/CONTINGENCY PLAN:

I WILL EMBODY "LOVE" BY: (SPECIFIC ACTIONS)

I FEEL EXCITED FOR/I FEEL APPREHENSIVE ABOUT:

THOUGHT DOWNLOAD:

Evening

EVENING (DATE:)

THE 1 THING I DID TODAY THAT SCARED ME

TODAY I LEARNED/EXPERIENCED:

I AM PROUD OF MYSELF FOR:

THE THINGS I COULD WORK ON DOING BETTER ARE:

I AM BLESSED BECAUSE:

THOUGHT DOWNLOAD:

Morning

MORNING (DATE:)

MY INTENTIONS/GOALS FOR TODAY ARE:
-
-
-

TODAY, I AM THANKFUL FOR:
-
-
-
-
-

POSSIBLE OBSTACLES:

PREVENTATIVE/CONTINGENCY PLAN:

I WILL EMBODY "LOVE" BY: (SPECIFIC ACTIONS)

I FEEL EXCITED FOR/I FEEL APPREHENSIVE ABOUT:

THOUGHT DOWNLOAD:

Evening

EVENING (DATE:)

THE 1 THING I DID TODAY THAT SCARED ME

TODAY I LEARNED/EXPERIENCED:

I AM PROUD OF MYSELF FOR:

THE THINGS I COULD WORK ON DOING BETTER ARE:

I AM BLESSED BECAUSE:

THOUGHT DOWNLOAD:

Morning

MORNING (DATE:)

MY INTENTIONS/GOALS FOR TODAY ARE:

-
-
-

TODAY, I AM THANKFUL FOR:

-
-
-
-
-

POSSIBLE OBSTACLES:

PREVENTATIVE/CONTINGENCY PLAN:

I WILL EMBODY "LOVE" BY: (SPECIFIC ACTIONS)

I FEEL EXCITED FOR/I FEEL APPREHENSIVE ABOUT:

THOUGHT DOWNLOAD:

Evening

EVENING (DATE:)

THE 1 THING I DID TODAY THAT SCARED ME

TODAY I LEARNED/EXPERIENCED:

I AM PROUD OF MYSELF FOR:

THE THINGS I COULD WORK ON DOING BETTER ARE:

I AM BLESSED BECAUSE:

THOUGHT DOWNLOAD:

Morning

MORNING (DATE:)

MY INTENTIONS/GOALS FOR TODAY ARE:
-
-
-

TODAY, I AM THANKFUL FOR:
-
-
-
-
-

POSSIBLE OBSTACLES:

PREVENTATIVE/CONTINGENCY PLAN:

I WILL EMBODY "LOVE" BY: (SPECIFIC ACTIONS)

I FEEL EXCITED FOR/I FEEL APPREHENSIVE ABOUT:

THOUGHT DOWNLOAD:

Evening

EVENING (DATE:)

THE 1 THING I DID TODAY THAT SCARED ME

TODAY I LEARNED/EXPERIENCED:

I AM PROUD OF MYSELF FOR:

THE THINGS I COULD WORK ON DOING BETTER ARE:

I AM BLESSED BECAUSE:

THOUGHT DOWNLOAD:

Made in the USA
Coppell, TX
17 February 2022